# Empathy and Resistance

# Empathy and Resistance

KRISTINA LUNZ

Translated by Nicola Barfoot

polity

Originally published in German as *Empathie und Widerstand* © by Ullstein Buchverlage GmbH, Berlin. Published in 2024 by Ullstein Verlag

This English translation © Polity Press, 2026

The translation of this book was supported by a grant from the Goethe-Institut.

Polity Press
65 Bridge Street
Cambridge CB2 1UR, UK

Polity Press
111 River Street
Hoboken, NJ 07030, USA

ISBN-13: 978-1-5095-7032-4 – hardback
ISBN-13: 978-1-5095-7033-1 – paperback

A catalogue record for this book is available from the British Library.

Library of Congress Control Number: 2025937029

Typeset in 11 on 14pt Warnock Pro
by Cheshire Typesetting Ltd, Cuddington, Cheshire
Printed and bound in Great Britain by CPI Group (UK) Ltd, Croydon.

The publisher has used its best endeavours to ensure that the URLs for external websites referred to in this book are correct and active at the time of going to press. However, the publisher has no responsibility for the websites and can make no guarantee that a site will remain live or that the content is or will remain appropriate.

Every effort has been made to trace all copyright holders, but if any have been overlooked the publisher will be pleased to include any necessary credits in any subsequent reprint or edition.

For further information on Polity, visit our website:

# Contents

# Acknowledgements

Many people have contributed their understanding, knowledge, expertise and passion to bring this book into existence in its present form. I am deeply grateful to them.

My greatest thanks go to my two editors, Silvie Horch and Heike Wolter. Thank you for helping me to give birth to this book. Having the chance to work with you again has not only given me a great deal of joy but has also allowed me to grow. I look forward to many more joint projects in future! Thanks also to Nathanael Stute for your valuable support in the editing process. And thank you to my publisher, Ullstein, and the fantastic team I've had the privilege of working with.

I would like to extend my sincere thanks to my British publisher, Polity Press, for bringing the English edition of this book to life. A special thank you to John Thompson and Elise Heslinga, as well as to Nicola Barfoot, who did a fantastic job translating the book.

Huge thanks to the following people who have, in very different ways, supported me and the development of the book – be it with valuable ideas, proofreading of the manuscript or allowing me to include their portraits: Ailbhe Smyth, Beatrice Fihn, Beggymaus Seemann, Bianca Praetorins, Düzen Tekkal,

Enissa Amani, Gloria Steinem, Ijad Madisch, Janina Hell, Jutta von Falkenhausen, Laura Fischer, Luisa Neubauer, Navid Norouzi (love you <3), Nina Bernarding, Stellah Bosire, Thomas Grischko and Yara Hoffmann. I thank you all from the bottom of my heart.

# 1

# How I found my compass

When Putin put his nuclear forces on high alert, Anne Hathaway was waiting for us. It was February 2022, and the Oscar-winning US actor had a front-row seat at the fashion show of a famous Italian designer. I'd been invited to Milan by the same fashion label, as one of twelve ambitious, independent women from all over the world chosen to front a campaign for female empowerment.

The other women and I were meeting Hathaway in the hotel bar before the show. The plan was to walk to the fashion show together, through streets lined with paparazzi, photographers, fans and onlookers. It was Fashion Week, and the Italian metropolis was pulsating with life and glamour. But I arrived at the meeting point late, with traces of tears on my face. One of the label's managers noticed immediately and gave me a sceptical look. 'Are you excited to be walking to the show with Hathaway and the others?' she asked. My voice trembled as I explained: 'Putin has just put his nuclear forces on high alert.'

It was a Sunday afternoon, the weekend after 24 February 2022, the date when the Russian leader had given the order to launch a large-scale attack on Ukraine. As a direct reaction to this, at a special session of the German parliament, Chancellor

Olaf Scholz had announced a *Zeitenwende* (a new epoch or turning point) and a special fund of 100 billion euros for the German armed forces.[*]

My own personal state of emergency was exacerbated by the fact that my first book, *The Future of Foreign Policy Is Feminist*, had just been published. And of all the dates that could have happened it had to be that fateful 24 February, the day of Putin's invasion. In response I was subjected to antifeminist and misogynist insults, defamation and derision. The general tenor was 'What can feminism do to stop Putin's weapons?' I was also deeply shaken by Russia's violence and the fear of escalation – and now I found myself sitting in front of the catwalk in ridiculously expensive (borrowed) clothes. To make matters worse, I made myself unpopular by refusing to pose for a photo with the other women and the famous fashion designer. It was a 'once-in-a-lifetime' event, but with my emotional state mirroring the state of the world, I just couldn't.

Two years later, in summer 2024, a woman stood up next to me. She took the microphone and said: 'I went into the jungle to meet the tigers. Because if you want peace, you have to hold the enemy's hand.' She spoke as the mother of a Sri Lankan soldier who had been kidnapped during the country's decades-long civil war. The 'tigers' were the paramilitary Tamil Tigers, fighting for the independence of the Tamil-dominated north and east of Sri Lanka. Her son was fighting against them.

---

[*] The idea of making or buying more and more weapons is contrary to all my convictions. I do believe that it's right, in our hypermilitarized world, to supply weapons in the short term, to save, support and protect people who are threatened. But at the same time, we have to find more sustainable solutions in the medium and long term. Because weapons alone have never made peace, they have always achieved the opposite. Examples of sustainable solutions are special funds for crisis prevention, (nuclear) disarmament, strengthening international law and human rights, adapting to and containing the climate crisis, supporting human rights defenders and (feminist) civil society worldwide. See Kristina Lunz, *The Future of Foreign Policy Is Feminist*, trans. Nicola Barfoot, Cambridge: Polity, 2023, p. 15.

I was in Tirana, the capital of Albania, with around a hundred women from all over the world – Syria, Yemen, Egypt, Liberia, Colombia and Afghanistan, to name but a few – for a peacebuilding conference. The work on peace and security was our common denominator. It was brutally and painfully underlined by the presence and the testimony of the Palestinian participants, who were – and still are – affected by war and displacement.

A few days later I was invited to the German–Israeli programme of a German foundation. The participants from both nations came from business, politics and NGOs. During our one-week stay in Berlin we came to trust each other, especially as we shared personal stories – both descriptions of the terrible attack by Hamas on 7 October 2023, from the Israeli perspective, and accounts of Israel's subsequent operations in the Gaza Strip.

In Israel men are generally required to do three years of compulsory military service, and women two years. Reservists – including some of the participants in the exchange programme – are then deployed in times of crisis and war.

My everyday life is marked by contrasting worlds, contradictions and conflicting perspectives. I've described my experiences in Milan, Tirana and Berlin to give an impression of these contrasts. In the morning I go to meetings with the German armed forces or at the Chancellery in Berlin, where the importance of increased armament* is invariably emphasized (with no mention of a long-term, non-reactive strategy). In the afternoon I talk about human security with groups of international experts, who observe the global arms race with growing concern.

It's a huge challenge to maintain my openness towards different perspectives, experiences and needs, while drawing my

---

* Or, as they call it there, 'equipping the Bundeswehr'. Often the different worlds don't even agree on terminology.

own red lines – on the violation of human rights, for example – more and more clearly. For me, this describes the balancing act between empathy and resistance, a dance between different, sometimes contradictory perspectives and clearly defined boundaries. Sometimes I dance with self-confidence, but at other times I'm still a learner and unsure of my steps.

In this ongoing process my aim is always to retain a little of this uncertainty and never be completely confident about my own attitude. This enables me to keep learning and developing. In my view, maintaining a degree of doubt about your own opinion and repeatedly questioning your own position is the highest form of personal maturity – especially if you can still stand up for the things you believe in.

In this dance between empathy and resistance, in the attempt to make our society more just, it's helpful to remember that politics is largely a matter of psychology. Politics arises in the process of negotiation between different emotions and needs, and has much less to do with rational behaviour than you might think. Maren Urner, a German neuroscientist and the author of *Radikal emotional – Wie Gefühle Politik machen* (Radically emotional: how feelings make politics), writes that humans are always emotional and that emotions are always political: 'Everything that defines our coexistence and thus the political sphere, which [. . .] is present always and everywhere, is shaped by emotions.'[1]

This also applies to political action in exceptional circumstances. From a historical perspective, wars are usually nothing but immature reactions by hyperemotional, aggressive men with too much power and too little emotional control. So wars have nothing to do with strength, but are a sign of emotional immaturity and weakness of character.

I gained my first insights into the importance of psychology for politics in 2013, when I took part in a three-week summer school on political psychology at Stanford University. I listened to lectures about what impedes successful peace negotiations, how social influence affects decision-making, and what conditions are needed for cooperation. I heard about predictors of collective violence and protest, learned useful facts about group dynamics, and studied the impact of media reporting on voting behaviour. Not only did I feel, for the first time, that it made sense to be doing a master's degree in international politics after my bachelor's in psychology; I also learned that emotions determine our politics.

Everything I've learned so far about communication, emotion and human interaction – especially in my years of work with my psychological coach – helps me to cope with the turbulent times we live in. The art of good communication is based on openness, attentiveness and understanding, the basic ingredients for empathy. These tools have helped me to de-escalate almost any conflict without having to give up my position or accept injustices.

When societies are in flux, the world is full of challenges and humanity faces a multitude of unresolved questions, it is essential to be able to tolerate different feelings and conditions simultaneously. Psychologists have a term for this ability to manoeuvre in a complex word: ambiguity tolerance. The key is not just to live with (or at best accept) the existence of many different and even contradictory views; it is to recognize that this diversity is not threatening, but enriching.

In a complex world there are no simple answers. Some people try to persuade us that these simple answers do exist. But these are populists – on both sides of the political spectrum. They lack ambiguity tolerance. In a book entitled *Dummheit* (Stupidity) the Austrian psychiatrist Heidi Kastner puts it as follows: 'Tolerating ambivalence and inconsistency is one of the essential developmental tasks in the process of maturation, a process that many people, to all appearances, have not gone through.'[2]

In this book I focus on nuances. This is about different feelings and truths which must be tolerated simultaneously, even those that initially seem contradictory, such as anger and optimism. For me, these two feelings are the foundation for empathy and resistance, the core elements that make up my (socio-)political stance.

This world full of complexity and challenges is quite different from the one I grew up in. I had a very sheltered childhood in a small village – fewer than a hundred inhabitants – in northern Bavaria. Both families of grandparents were farmers; my grandmother (who still lives in the village, along with other family members) actually has the surname 'Bauer', meaning farmer. Growing up in our village of farmers (as my family used to describe it) was a very special and wonderful experience, full of nature and love. I looked after my cat, my pygmy rabbit and our other rabbits. We were always thrilled to discover baby rabbits in the hutch. Their eyes still closed at first, they snuggled together in their nest of straw and hay, mixed with fur plucked from the mother rabbit's own body. I was even more delighted when we heard the mewling of kittens in the barn in spring and autumn and, following the sound, found the babies of the stray village cats in the hay. My childhood memories include fields and woods, the brook, the stable, meadows and animals. Politics meant nothing to me then. It was a lovely, free childhood. Often my twin brother and I went out with the other village kids, spent the day roaming the woods and meadows, and didn't come home until early evening.

But from my teens on I felt increasingly uncomfortable. I struggled with the norms of my little world, such as the idea that men should – and did – call the shots. The mayor, the priest, the master baker and the school principal, the pub owner and the head of the village council, the fire chief and the head of the sports club – every single position of power was filled by men. At the Sunday match the whole community cheered for the men's football team. All the admiration and respect went to the men, while women carried out unpaid care work at home, looking after the children and running the household.

This respect was so strong that some of these men felt they could overstep women's and girls' boundaries with impunity. Such incidents might happen in the driving instructor's car or at village festivals and sports days. At some point I wasn't prepared to accept this any more. I wanted to resist. I wanted to get away, and university offered me the escape route I needed, even if I initially found it hard to imagine a world outside my village. I studied psychology for my bachelor's degree, then secured scholarships that enabled me to complete two master's programmes, one in London and one in Oxford.

And suddenly I found myself caught between two worlds. One was my home, my Bavarian village; the other was this increasingly international, sometimes elitist world where, time and time again, I was made to feel that I didn't really belong. I wore the wrong clothes, I hadn't read enough books, I just didn't quite fit in. My experiences suddenly became political, and I began to write about what it was like to come to Oxford as a working-class country girl. I realized that the elites needed to become more diverse.[3]

As these worlds collided, I came to question the traditional, supposedly natural rules more and more. I became a feminist and an activist. I was driven by a mixture of empathy and resistance to blatant injustices. I empathized with those who were marginalized or suffered from unjust structures. And my rage gave me the energy to rebel against these structures. Rather than wallowing in my anger, I wanted to use it constructively. 'Anger at injustice and inequality is in many ways exactly like fuel,' writes Rebecca Traister in *Good and Mad: The Revolutionary Power of Women's Anger*.[4] Traister shows how women's anger releases transformative energy, from the suffragettes to the legendary Black civil rights campaigner Rosa Parks, and from #MeToo to the 2017 Women's March in Washington, DC.

In summer 2014 I was full of anger. I was no longer prepared to accept what was then seen as normality: the daily
sexualization and degradation of women in what was, at the
time, Europe's biggest-selling newspaper. The specific trigger
was a front page of *Bild*, the German equivalent of *The Sun*. It
showed photos of the cleavage of successful, famous women
and invited readers to vote for the 'best bosom on German
TV'. Disgusted by the degrading treatment of these celebrities
and of women in general, I responded with a campaign against
*Bild*. Over 60,000 people signed my petition, demanding that
'It's time all people were treated with the same respect in *Bild*
and *bild.de*: women are not society's sex objects!' Suddenly I
was giving interviews and getting up on stage to speak about
my campaign. In 2018 the '*Bild* girl', the equivalent of *The Sun*'s
'Page 3 girl', was discontinued. The tabloid's explanation was
that 'many women see these pictures as offensive and degrading, both in our editorial team and among our female readers'.[5]
Various media outlets saw a connection to my campaign.

A year after my petition there was a mass outbreak of sexualized assaults against women by men on the night of New
Year's Eve 2015 in Cologne. I felt strongly that – whatever the
specific events of that night – it was wrong and hypocritical
to claim that it was only the 'other' men, those of non-white
skin colour and non-German origin, who were guilty of sexual
violence in Germany. This is a global problem, so it's a German
problem too. It's a problem that exists in every country in the
world that has men in it – in villages, in cities, everywhere.

Working with twenty other women and non-binary activists, I launched the campaign 'Against sexualized violence and
racism. Always. Anywhere. #Ausnahmslos' ('NoExcuses'). We
formulated fourteen demands for politicians, society and the
media. We wrote: 'It is harmful for all of us if feminism is
exploited by extremists to incite against certain ethnicities,
as is currently being done in the discussion surrounding
the incidents in Cologne. It is wrong to highlight sexualised

violence only when the perpetrators are allegedly the per-ceived "others."[6] We were not prepared to let the racist and populist positions of the AfD (Alternative for Germany, parts of which have been officially designated as far-right extrem-ist) go uncontested. Our demands made it onto the online front pages of major German news media, and we received the Clara Zetkin Prize for political intervention, awarded by the German Left Party and named after a famous early twentieth-century communist, pacifist and feminist. It was the first big campaign by intersectional feminists in Germany to attract serious media attention. We were just twenty-one women who refused to keep quiet any longer, and we made feminist history.

One thing I learned during this campaign was that, in Germany at the beginning of 2016, a woman's 'no' was not enough to justify a prosecution for rape. Scandalous. Until 1997, men had been legally permitted to rape their wives. Until 2016, a rape victim – a woman, in more than 90 per cent of cases – had to prove that she had resisted her rapist physically.

I worked with UN Women Germany on a voluntary basis, helping to develop their 'No Means No' campaign. Many other women's rights organizations had also been fighting for years to change the law on sexual offences. We joined forces, wrote articles and commentaries, lobbied members of parliament, drew up reports, gave interviews. In March 2016, in an article for *Zeit Online*, I wrote: 'No means no – it's high time. There is no rational argument against it, except the desperate attempt to uphold a system in which the rights of men count more than those of women.'[7] Law professors and lawyers intimated that I should hold my tongue; as a person with no legal train-ing, I clearly had no idea what I was talking about. I was, they suggested, trying to turn the bedroom into a crime scene. As if it hadn't been exactly that for many women, for centuries! The statements of those law experts showed me what happens when only the male point of view is regarded as relevant, as has been the case since time immemorial. Despite all these attempts at intimidation, we won: the law on sexual offences was changed in July 2016, and no now means no.

Strengthened by my experiences, I began an international career, working in Bogotá in Colombia, in New York and in Yangon, the former capital of Myanmar. I worked for various organizations, including the United Nations, in the areas of peacebuilding and women's and human rights. Here too, I found myself questioning the narratives, modes of action and priorities of actors in diplomacy and foreign policy. I found it strange and surprising that economic interests were often given more weight than human rights, and that weapons of mass destruction were regarded as guarantors of security. How was it possible that, despite widening international conflicts and wars and the increasing militarization of international spending, virtually no one was willing to acknowledge the empirically proven connection between more militarization, more wars and more victims?

So I gathered all my expertise and my courage and in 2018, Nina Bernarding and I founded the non-profit enterprise Centre for Feminist Foreign Policy (CFFP) in Berlin. I wrote the first book on the subject to be published worldwide, the above-mentioned *The Future of Foreign Policy Is Feminist*, which became a bestseller in Germany and was translated into English. In autumn 2021 the coalition agreement of the newly formed German government, consisting of the Social Democrats (SPD), the Greens and the Liberals (FDP), contained a commitment to feminist foreign policy. In March 2023 the German foreign minister Annalena Baerbock presented the feminist foreign policy strategy of the German foreign office. CFFP – which had grown to fifteen staff members by that time – advised the ministry. I had the opportunity to share the stage with the minister on the day the strategy was presented. At an evening event at the Munich Security Conference in 2023, Baerbock said that if it were not for my work, our work, Germany would never have had a feminist foreign policy.

My journey from the village into the world was not yet over. But I had reached a milestone, where I felt that my actions were having an effect. The things I was doing – in collaboration with others – were changing our society. Today my everyday working life includes attending the UN General Assembly High-Level Week, NATO conferences and other such events. I give expert advice to embassies, ministries and governments, and I work with human rights defenders and civil societies worldwide.

Our work at CFFP involves calling into question doctrines and positions in foreign and security policy that have gone unchallenged for decades or even centuries. We seek to change the structures, priorities and financial decision-making processes, and thus the institutions themselves. We develop countermodels to militarized masculinity, the logic of nuclear deterrence and the arms industry. These traditional systems are so robust that all our successes and interventions are only small steps on the path towards a better situation. They are incremental changes, gradual adaptations or advances over time. But the suffering experienced worldwide demands many, many more steps. Climate change and the resulting natural disasters, war and increasing authoritarianism, all these things cry out for action.

I feel as though I've gradually become better equipped for my day-to-day work, which often feels like an unwinnable battle. I'm more productive and optimistic because I'm able to act with empathy, sensitivity and understanding, but at the same time I know when I have to set boundaries and put up resistance. In Kim Stanley Robinson's terrific novel *The Ministry for the Future*, the head of the ministry, Mary, initially doubts her suitability for the position. She thinks the feisty Tatiana would suit the role better. But Tatiana replies: 'You have to get people to listen to you before you can make your case. That's what you do – people listen to you. Then we can go to work.'[8]

How can we go to work to change the world? This is a question I also ask myself on a regular basis. How far can we challenge the people in positions of power and at the same time maintain our access to and collaboration with them? We believe this is essential, since change can and must be pursued both inside and outside institutions.

If we want to promote changes in society and secure human rights for all, it is not enough to think and argue about content. If we really want to achieve something, it is equally important to cultivate our relationships with those we are interacting with. When people fight about an issue, this is mainly about emotions and emotional control, empathy, resistance and individual attitudes.

I believe it is crucial to meet other people and other positions with openness and a capacity for empathy. But that doesn't mean I have to find something positive about every person or attitude. I can, of course, start to take a more critical stance if the person I'm speaking to denies important principles such as human rights or refuses to recognize the humanity of all people. Attentiveness, understanding and empathy are very important, but that doesn't mean that every boundary can be crossed. It's vital to put up resistance if our own values are called into question.

When I helped to introduce the principle 'No means no' into German criminal law in 2016, my attitude was this: I could understand that some political actors and law scholars didn't support this change, because it was new. But there was simply no alternative to reforming paragraph 177 of the German criminal code. The rate of conviction for rape in Germany was only about 1 per cent, which meant that tens of thousands of women (since women make up the majority of rape victims) were failing to get justice. This was unacceptable.[9]

It may sound naïve, but I say this with absolute sincerity: I want to help to make the world – or at least the parts of society in which my actions can have an impact – fairer and less violent, and I want to get as many people behind me as I can. Or, to use the words of one of my role models, former US Supreme

Court judge Ruth Bader Ginsburg: 'Fight for the things that you care about, but do it in a way that will lead others to join you.'[10]

I firmly believe that a mixture of empathy, openness and attentiveness, coupled with clear boundaries and resistance to injustice, is a mode of action that many people can identify with.

\* \* \*

I am writing these lines from a privileged perspective. In times of a worldwide shift to the right and increasing dominance of authoritarian states, I see it as a privilege to live in a democracy. In 2023 71 per cent of the world's population lived in autocracies.[11] Despite the strong and extremely dangerous shift to the right in Germany and in Europe, coupled with increasing anti-semitism and anti-Muslim racism, Germany is, like large parts of Europe, still a democracy. This allows participation, even if it is hampered – as in other parts of the world – by deeply rooted structures of oppression and exclusion, such as racism, sexism and classism. It is participation that breathes life into democracy.

But how can positive change be achieved, if we have the freedom to attempt it? I have devoted my life to working for women's rights and human rights. As a (social) entrepreneur, author and activist, I use my influence and expertise. The challenges are enormous, but this makes my desire to improve social conditions all the stronger. What is needed is a moral compass, an attitude shaped by humanity and understanding, but which sets clear boundaries and achieves positive change. To accomplish this, empathy and resistance must coincide.

This book explains how this can work. Based on personal impressions and experiences, I explore how self-efficacy in our attitudes and actions can contribute to a fairer society. In the sixth chapter I present portraits of women who, with exactly this combination of empathy and resistance, have gained substantial social influence and changed the world for the better. Whether or not we've worked together personally, these women are my comrades-in-arms. In their successful battles for women's and human rights, health equity, nuclear disarmament and the liberalization of abortion, and against right-wing extremism, they're more than just fellow fighters, though – they're my role models. I've been learning from them for years and will continue to do so. As with many other noteworthy defenders of democracy and human rights, we can say: when they win, we all win.

# 2

# Empathy

*Empathy* refers to the fundamental ability to perceive and understand the emotions and motives of others. This includes the willingness to put ourselves in another person's place and comprehend their emotional state, without necessarily sharing it. Empathy enables us to develop compassion and understanding for the situation of others and to react appropriately. Three different forms of empathy have been identified: cognitive, emotional and behavioural.[1]

*Cognitive empathy* is the ability to comprehend another person's perspective on an intellectual level. It's about being open to another person's way of thinking and trying to understand it. This skill has no moral value – it's a strength that benefits both doctors and hardened criminals. *Emotional empathy* is the ability to sense and respond to another person's emotions. This includes sympathizing with joy, grief, anger, or other emotions that people may have. *Behavioural empathy* is the ability to react appropriately to the feelings and needs of others. This is about empathetic action and support, helping or comforting others in difficult situations.

For Heidi Kastner, the Austrian psychiatrist mentioned in chapter 1, emotional empathy is essential if we are to find real solutions to complex challenges. In her book *Dummheit* she argues that it is not stupid to demand a substantial change in existing conditions. It *is* stupid, however, to believe in quick and easy solutions: 'Real solutions would require more emotional empathy, that is, the ability to share others' feelings, to develop compassion, to act in their interests, and to make relationships equal, that is, not to do to others what we would not want to have done to us.'[2]

In 2015, just a few years before his death, the physicist Stephen Hawking said that of all human failings, the one he would most like to correct would be aggression.

> It may have had survival advantage in caveman days, to get more food, territory, or [a] partner with whom to reproduce, but now it threatens to destroy us all. A major nuclear war would be the end of civilization, and maybe the end of the human race. The quality I would most like to magnify is empathy. It brings us together in a peaceful, loving state.[3]

## Empathy is not a cure-all

Here I would disagree with Hawking, to some extent. An increase in empathy is not an end in itself – it does not automatically mean an increase in 'good', moral behaviour. Empathy – especially emotional empathy, i.e. the ability to feel what others are feeling – also has negative sides. Sometimes it can even stand in the way of justice, for example if we show more empathy towards one group of people than another and deny justice to the latter group as a result. As humans, we feel more empathy towards people who are (or appear to be) closer and more similar to us; people whose misfortune afflicts us more or whose war is geographically nearer to us; people with whom we are more closely connected emotionally. It's an extension of the obvious evolutionary fact that parents prioritize the protection and safety of their own children over others.

Whether consciously or unconsciously, we must constantly readjust our view of the world, with all its suffering, and weigh up whether to intervene or not. Without these filters we would be totally overwhelmed, every day of our lives; at a certain point, we'd become incapable of action. Imagine feeling the pain of all the children living in poverty, all the abused women, all the men affected by police brutality, all the victims of war, all the refugees, all those whose loved ones are dying. Sharing in the unfathomable suffering of all the people in the world just as much as we share the pain of our parents, children, best friends or partners would vastly exceed our capacity for empathy.

In *Against Empathy: The Case for Rational Compassion*[4] psychology professor Paul Bloom discusses the 'spotlight' function of empathy: we feel (emotional) empathy for those whose suffering we *are able* to focus our attention on. In personal relationships empathy can inspire compassion and protection, but in the larger context of the world it often means that certain people are overlooked. This is because fighting injustices demands attention, which is fuelled by empathy for a particular group of people. We empathize most strongly with those who are similar to us and whom we find attractive, while we often lack empathy for the many people who are different, distant or anonymous. As a result we sometimes become desensitized and unable (or unwilling) to see their suffering.

Outside the spotlight of attention and empathy there is darkness, which conceals the suffering of countless other people. These endless shadowy realms outside the spotlight consolidate forms of oppression such as sexism, for example when men in positions of power are more willing to provide funds for the interests and problems of men. Or racism, for example when our sympathy towards refugees depends on where they come from and how similar to us they are. As a result, European refugees are welcomed, while we let people from Africa and Asia drown in the Mediterranean in their thousands. When the psychological categorization of in-groups and out-groups ('us' and 'them') affects real-life political decision-making, for example when it leads to the inhumane treatment of refugees, the consequences can be deadly.

The 'spotlight' function provides us with one possible explanation, and can help us to counteract forms of discrimination such as sexism or racism. But this theory must not be permitted to excuse or legitimize inaction. For me, it leads to the following normative requirement: despite all psychological explanations, we must at least try to always have empathy for all people and their suffering.

Bloom's theory also allows us to refute the common assumption that conservative politicians are less empathetic than left-wing liberals. According to his explanation, empathy is just a function; it does not tell us how large the spotlight is, or which groups or categories it illuminates and which ones it leaves in the shadows. The difference is in the size of the in-group: for conservatives, this group is smaller, while liberal left-wing universalists would ideally like to expand the spotlight to the point where there is no longer any out-group.*

Fritz Breithaupt, a professor of cognitive science, has also written a book intended to 'free us from a simplistic view of empathy', since people 'do terrible things with and out of empathy'.[5] In *Die dunklen Seiten der Empathie* (The dark sides of empathy) the author describes the 'seemingly inhumane things that we do or feel, not although but because we have empathy'.[6] He discusses the ambivalent nature of empathy, which should never be seen as the sole basis for moral action.

---

* In his chapter on 'The politics of empathy' in *Against Empathy: The Case for Rational Compassion* (New York: Ecco, 2016), Paul Bloom explores whether liberals/people on the left are actually more empathetic than conservatives/those on the right. While there is some empirical evidence for this, the differences are not as significant as is sometimes assumed.

On the contrary, Breithaupt argues, empathy plays a central role in a number of highly problematic behaviours, such as terrorism, where one-sided empathy for one group legitimizes violence towards another one. The same goes for exploitation, harassment, or persistent oppression. To some extent, such behaviours can be explained by partisanship. Empathy for the situation of one group reduces our empathy for the other group; this can then lead to hasty judgements and unreflecting partisanship, which results in black-and-white thinking. Breithaupt writes that this dynamic of partisanship and empathy allows us to make rapid and firm decisions, intervene in conflicts and take clear positions. 'The more I feel the pain of the one side, the more I will stand up for them. Empathy thus legitimizes me in both positive and negative behaviour towards others.'[7] Conflicts are becoming more polarized and radicalized. This then paves the way for the very dark sides of empathy mentioned above. Terrorism is a particularly drastic case of polarization, based on the 'choice of a faction and the sympathy for a movement'.[8]

I am aware of the inadequacy of my own (and everyone else's) claims to morality, empathy and so on. My psychology degree was certainly useful, if not absolutely essential; it helped me to develop an awareness that, despite many a good intention, actual behaviour is usually anything but ideal. Even if we want to do the right thing, emotionality and one-sided empathy can thwart this intention. Or the sincere aspiration to be empathetic towards all people ultimately turns out to be fallible, time and time again. Successful and fair empathy is an intention that must overcome countless obstacles.

Empathy alone is not a good enough counsellor; it is not, in itself, a basis for moral behaviour. Hence the title of this book: *Empathy and Resistance*. I firmly believe that an increase in empathy alone cannot bring about the necessary social change. Empathy needs support but also opposition, and this is where resistance comes in.

To allow the necessary shifts between empathy and resistance, certain guiding principles are needed. For me, these are human rights, non-violence and universalism. Universalism is the conviction that certain principles, values, or norms – such as human rights – should apply to everyone, regardless of their origin, culture or other differences. The aim of the concept is to establish a generally accepted level of justice, rights or morality, which can be universally acknowledged and applied. So if people show the dark sides of empathy, violating human rights, deploying violence, or denying universalism, this is where empathy reaches its limits, in my view. This is the point where my understanding and sympathy for an attitude or position is replaced by inner resistance.

The role of power is also central to the question of how far my empathy should go, and where resistance should begin. In the contemporary feminist movement, as in the historical tradition of feminist thought, power is a key analytical tool. Who has the power to establish and disseminate narratives, make laws, control resources, and grant or deny rights? The answer to this determines which paths of intervention and protest can be taken to achieve more equality and justice.

Positions of power give people different options and levels of control. To this day, these positions of power – whether in politics, business or culture – are disproportionately in the hands of men, all over the world. For me, the position (of power) that a person holds influences the amount of empathy I approach them with. If a minister of justice blocks an increase in legal protections for women, I judge him harshly (showing resistance rather than empathy for his behaviour) and denounce him publicly. If a concerned father argues against women's rights because he fears that growing equality will mean a loss of privilege for his son, my response is different. My reasoning is that the minister's attitude has a much more serious impact on millions of women because of his position of power.

I believe it is important to differentiate between the person and the role. For example, I can take a hard line against justice ministers who deny women their rights, representatives of the arms industry who lobby against laws to control the export of weapons, or journalists who work for media outlets that harm our society. Yet at the same time I can feel empathy for these individuals as human beings.

These different elements help me to set my empathy compass. When is empathy productive, and when does it facilitate injustices, atrocities and human rights violations? If this occurs, I turn to resistance. But until it happens, I regard many aspects, components and derivatives of empathy as valuable. Empathy is not a silver bullet that can fix all the injustice and misery in the world on its own. But if we are ever to achieve the fairer and less violent utopia that I dream of, it is still highly relevant. On the following pages I will examine its diverse and complex characteristics.

## Openness, not judgement and condemnation

I'm aware that the word 'contempt' is a strong one, which is why I choose it with care. But in this case I think it's appropriate: I feel contempt for the tabloid *Bild* and the company that publishes it, Axel Springer SE. I despise this newspaper and this company for all the suffering they've inflicted, for many decades, on our society and on particular groups and individuals, especially women and people with a history of migration. The damage they've inflicted is so immense that I wish the newspaper and the company simply didn't exist.

My personal confrontation with *Bild* and Springer began, as described above, at the end of 2014, when I publicly opposed the paper's blatant sexism and demanded a respectful portrayal of women. The response of the editor at the time, Kai Diekmann, was exactly what the newspaper had always stood for: an aggressive personal counterattack, arrogant and disrespectful, aimed at discrediting me. Diekmann aggravated the situation further by stirring up his tens of thousands of Twitter followers against me. The devastating online violence I faced as a result included insults, sexualized digital violence, rape fantasies directed at me and threats to my family.

Over the years, journalists from *Bild* and *Welt*, another newspaper owned by Springer, continued to publish defamatory statements about me, some of which I was able to contain with the help of lawyers and other support. The law was on my side here; in some cases the journalists had no choice but to retract and correct their false statements.

My attitude to this media company has been reinforced by women I know who have been directly affected by the behaviour of Diekmann's power-abusing successor, Julian Reichelt. My knowledge of how the company's top management dealt with the scandal at the time has further intensified my contempt.

A chance encounter with Springer's head of communications in a Berlin bar one night, at the time when I was writing this book, did not improve my impression of the company. It speaks volumes when someone in this position starts to talk about women as 'bitches' – and to disparage me as an intern – within moments of beginning a conversation.

I repeat: I have nothing but contempt for *Bild*, and I wish this newspaper and the company that owns it did not exist in their present, powerful form.

Over the years, however, I've met many people at Springer, holding a wide range of positions and responsibilities, some of them influential figures. When I first met one of these people, my underlying attitude made me very sceptical. For many years, the person in question has been good friends with someone very close to me. We had long conversations, in which I explained my position and they explained theirs. It turned out that we were not as far apart as my intuitive scepticism had made me assume. We both wanted to criticize the same structures and change them if possible; the only difference was that one of us wanted to do it from the outside and the other from the inside.

The question is whether and to what extent working within problematic structures ultimately reinforces them, even if we hope to change them. This is an important question, which has cropped up many times in my life in various contexts. When it comes to Springer and its senior management, unfortunately, my scepticism about the possibility of real change from within is stronger than my optimism.

The other person saw this differently; they had different convictions, which resulted in different decisions. My initial prejudice changed, along with my inclination to judge and condemn this person's actions. Since I now understand them and their motivations better, I'm grateful that my openness gradually got the better of my erroneous preconceptions. Today I recognize the value and significance of this person's work and am extremely appreciative of our relationship.

Empathy demands, first and foremost, that we switch off all judgement and condemnation. Being empathetic means acknowledging the full humanity of every person, with all the attendant implications. If we succeed in accepting, without prejudice, that every person has their own experiences and realities, then we can say we're empathizing with them – even if their reality is different from ours.

Many years ago I consciously resolved not to automatically judge or condemn when I hear about the ideas, actions and views of others. If anything, judgement and condemnation should be the last step. It isn't easy to keep this resolution. None of us manage to go through life without judging or condemning anyone. But we can all make a conscious effort to approach others with empathy and openness. I believe that gossip and slander say more about the speaker than the subject.

Kindness, warmth and openness are directly linked to the desire not to speak ill of others. Together they indicate a fundamental willingness to empathize with others, to put ourselves in their place. I personally look up to people who have this attitude. Mother Teresa is believed to have said: 'If you judge people, you have no time to love them.' Heads and hearts that are busy judging and condemning others will have difficulty showing empathy towards them.

But if I realize that the person I'm dealing with is arguing or acting inhumanely, and if it's clear that they're not going to change, then judging them becomes an obligation and resistance an imperative. This too must be clear: the effort to avoid judging and condemning others must not lead us to show openness and misguided tolerance towards violations of human rights.

## Humanity

Not long ago, while scrolling through social media, I came across an anecdote that I can't get out of my head:

> During the Vietnam War, a man stood in front of the White House every evening holding a candle. Once a reporter went up to him and asked: 'Sir, do you really believe your little protest will change anything?' And he replied: 'Oh, I don't do this to change the country. I do this so the country won't change me.'[9]

This touching story illustrates the importance of humanity and individual responsibility in the midst of current conflicts and social challenges. It shows us that our first concern should always be our own attitude. We don't know whether we can change others. But we can and should take responsibility, at all times, for our actions and our impact. This should come from within us, and not be imposed from outside. We always have the power to change ourselves, and, ideally, our being and doing will also have a positive influence on others and therefore society. The man with the candle illustrates the power of individual humanity and the importance of fighting for what we see as good and right, even in adverse circumstances. The anecdote highlights the need to hold on to our own values and remain unswayed by external influences.

Since we're all humans, it might seem that humanity would come naturally to us. But 'humanity' relates to two different adjectives, 'human' and 'humane'. 'Human' describes typical characteristics of the human race, such as human emotions, human behaviour and so on. 'Humane', on the other hand, refers to empathy, kindness and consideration for other people (and other living creatures), especially those in difficult or vulnerable situations. Humanity, as well as being a synonym for humankind, can mean both humanness and humaneness.

As I see it, prioritizing humanity – in the sense of humaneness – means first and foremost seeing every person as a human being, instead of pigeonholing them or getting tangled up in questions of identity. Humanity is more important than identity. Acknowledging the humanity (i.e. humanness) of every single person also means understanding that we all have individual realities on the basis of identity categories such as gender, race and social origin. These make up the diversity and depth of our humanness. This universalism is traditionally one of the fundamental pillars of left-wing thinking, as the author Susan Neiman emphasizes.[10]

One principle of universalism is alliances. International solidarity includes a sense of connection and support for others, such as freedom fighters in South Africa or civil rights campaigners in the US. This distinguishes the left wing from the right wing: the latter often doesn't recognize any connections or commitments beyond its in-groups.

As Neiman sees it, left-wing international solidarity encompasses the whole globe. What unites us, she argues, is not blood, but the conviction that humans are deeply connected with one another in various ways, despite the differences in time and space that separate us. In her book *Left Is Not Woke*, Neiman notes with concern that a large part of today's left is moving away from universalism and towards tribalism, thus converging with right-wing thinking.[11]

I try to resist this tendency. My political convictions are based on a radical universalism.* I believe that all humans deserve my full respect regardless of their identity markers, and I demand the realization of human rights for all. The opposition between in-group and out-group must never be privileged over the acknowledgement of universal dignity, and identity must never outweigh humanity.

*          *          *

On 7 October 2023 the terrorist organization Hamas committed the worst massacre of Jews since the Holocaust. This heralded the start of the brutal Israeli military operation in the Gaza Strip, under the far-right government of Benjamin Netanyahu, in which countless Palestinians have been killed.

In the days and weeks after the Hamas attack, during Israel's ongoing retaliation, the idea of humanity has been very important to me as I attempt to find a position. Such a position has to be based on universalism and thus on the humanity (i.e. humanness) of those affected. At the same time, it must unequivocally acknowledge the intolerable pain of the civilians in Israel and Gaza. Ideologies, propaganda and the misguided tendency to equate people with their political leaders blind us and contribute to a situation where we no longer see the humanity of one side, the Palestinians or the Jews. I see it like this: if we grieve more for certain human lives than others, based on the actions of those people's governments or the attitude of our own government, this is a victory for propaganda.

---

* They are partly inspired by the book of the same name by Omri Boehm: *Radical Universalism*, New York: New York Review Books, 2025.

In October 2023 the Israeli international law expert Michael Sfard wrote: 'Being humane is hard work. Remaining humane in the face of inhumane cruelty is far more difficult.' In the same article he makes a similar point to my argument earlier in this section, that humaneness – contrary to our intuitive assumption – is not a natural human trait. 'Much more natural is the desire to take revenge, to blame everyone on the other side, to drop thousands of bombs on them, to erase them from the face of the earth. Human history is full of examples, and apparently we haven't learned a thing.'[12]

Very few of us have the wisdom of that man who stood in front of the White House with a candle during the Vietnam War. Very few of us have really understood the truth: humanity starts with me, but it is always focused on others.


## Growth

An important aspect of empathy is to allow and foster growth. This applies to our own behaviour, capabilities and coping strategies, but also to our interactions with others and our own (political) stance.

Growth is often preceded by growing pains, however. In my case they manifest as a feeling of being out of balance, torn between different positions. I sleep badly; I feel restless, anxious and uncertain. You might say that my seabed – as a metaphor for my underlying emotional state – is churned up. Throughout my life I've tried to keep this metaphorical seabed calm, however bad the weather, even if there's a storm brewing or waves crashing on the surface.

By drawing clear boundaries and living in harmony with my needs, I generally succeed in maintaining a calm and balanced sense of self. However challenging the management and growth of my organization is, however much flak I'm bombarded with from the outside, however overloaded my calendar is, and whatever demands people are making of me, my top priority is always to keep my seabed calm.

But sometimes I don't succeed. Again and again I experience phases of growing pains, in which I feel that this one knot, the knot of growth, is so big that I need new coping strategies and skills if I want to find a healthy and sustainable way to deal with the current challenges. At moments like these I feel like a battered boxer hanging on the ropes.

At one point I actually felt an almost irresistible urge to close my organization and withdraw from public life and from the constant battle for women's and human rights. It was all too much for me, especially the digital violence and the judgements of the public. At first I wanted to give up. But then I learned to acknowledge and accept that I'd taken a hit and was struggling, but that it was OK to be in that position. I realized that I could rely on myself and that I had all the skills in me that I needed to get out of this situation. In retrospect this low point really helped me to understand and admit to myself and others that all forms of experience, even unpleasant ones, can be important and valuable, and that we can learn and grow from them.

Over the years, I've learned to identify such phases of growth in myself, and this has also made me more sympathetic and sensitive to the growth of others. Growth can mean developing by interacting with others; it can mean becoming more resilient, acquiring new abilities and coping strategies, adapting and refining our own political position, and much more.

After growth, a certain part of us is no longer the same as it was before. And that's fantastic, because it shows that we have the capacity to change and develop. I am most certainly not the same person I was a few years ago. As a result of growth, I occasionally end up apologizing to people close to me for my previous behaviour. It means I've changed and I've learned from the past.

In recent years a lot of my personal growth has had to do with socio-political positions. This is largely due to the fact that I'm always meeting new, inspiring people, from whom I learn a great deal – whether it be from their experiences, their attitudes, or their abilities. By keeping my ears and my heart open, I generally manage to take away something valuable from every encounter.

Often when I spend time with friends or acquaintances, they say at the end of the conversation: 'Oh, I've been talking the whole time, you hardly got a word in edgewise.' At moments like these I can sincerely reassure them that this really isn't a problem for me. I like listening and I'm good at paying attention. It's great for me: every time someone else talks, I have an opportunity to discover something new. When we ourselves speak, we only hear what we already know. The experiences of others, especially if they differ from my own, can make me rethink and adjust my own position – and grow as a person.

In my early twenties, for example, I thought that women's quotas were unnecessary and that anyone could achieve their goals regardless of their gender or social origin. This belief was strongly shaped by my conservative socialization in childhood. In my family, the principle of merit was important: my father, the son of a poor farming family, was the first in his family and his village to attend a *Realschule* and attain more than the most basic level of secondary schooling. His social advancement was a source of great pride and undoubtedly also influenced my own path in life.*

It took a few years before I began to question my convictions and look more closely at the experiences of those affected and the evidence. I realized then that the 'merit principle' is an illusion. It's a common narrative that rewards and advantages

---

* I wish he'd been able to see more of the path that brought me to this point. Unfortunately he died in 2014.

in society are distributed on the basis of merit or performance. But this idea not only excludes many people (such as people doing care work, which is often undervalued in a patriarchal society) or disadvantages them (e.g. people with disabilities). It also masks injustices such as discrimination, oppression and privilege.

Growth is about keeping an open mind and learning new things, but also 'unlearning' old things. From a feminist and justice-oriented perspective, this unlearning is crucial. It enables us to let go of narratives and structures that have been established for decades or even centuries, and to pave the way for a fairer future. In 2022 I contributed to an anthology of essays called *Unlearn Patriarchy*,[13] where we, the authors, did exactly this, rethinking topics such as love, family, sexuality, power, politics and work.

## Peacebuilding

One of the hardest but most important tasks for our society is peacebuilding. Peacebuilders face up to the challenge of resolving conflicts within societies and between nations. Peacebuilding is a complex process which aims to create a lasting peace and prevent the resurgence of violence.

When I talk about peace, I mean *positive* peace: a state that goes beyond the absence of violence. Unfortunately, peacetime does not automatically mean that everyone – especially those who suffer from structural violence such as sexism or racism – can live in peace and freedom. Thus peace should not be understood simply as the absence of war (*negative* peace). Real, positive peace requires the end of structural violence and disadvantage, including poverty, hunger, social injustice and inequality.

Peacebuilders work at various levels to promote peace and non-violence in societies. This includes peace education and conflict prevention, conflict resolution between opposing parties, mediation, post-conflict reconstruction and the resolution of socio-economic injustices. Their educational work focuses on restoring and fostering social cohesion and thus building resilient societies, which can manage their disputes peacefully and without violence.

In the last few years my work has given me the opportunity to meet numerous peacebuilders from different parts of the world: Myanmar, Colombia, Libya, Afghanistan, Ukraine and other countries and regions. Besides non-violence, one of their basic principles is always empathy. But this empathy is not uncontrolled and undirected. Unfiltered empathy, as we have seen above, can lead to partisanship. This exacerbates conflicts rather than resolving them. For peacebuilders, empathy serves to stress the humanity of *all* the parties in a conflict.

One of these peacebuilders is Sanam Naraghi-Anderlini. Sanam was born into the Iranian elite, emigrated to the UK during the Islamic Revolution of 1979, and now commutes between London and the US, where she works as the founder and director of the International Civil Society Action Network. In the last thirty years, she has actively supported numerous peace processes, including those in Somalia, Nepal and Afghanistan. I met Sanam in 2017 at the Commission on the Status of Women, the most renowned and important international women's rights conference, which takes place annually at the United Nations in New York.

In a panel discussion she explained that the UN's Women, Peace and Security (WPS) agenda is misunderstood if its practical impact is to bring more women into military service (something that many countries have in fact pushed for). Instead, she argued, we must eliminate destructive, militaristic structures, so that neither sons nor daughters have to join the military and fight in violent conflicts. The aim is to prevent conflicts, not to make them more equal. WPS encompasses a whole cluster of resolutions of the UN Security Council. These are concerned with the role of women in peacebuilding and the importance of women's security for lasting peace.* Sanam is one of the 'mothers' of the agenda, having co-authored the first resolution in the late 1990s.

For Sanam, peacebuilding means seeking the humanity in the 'other', and creating a space for dialogue, in which violence is replaced by non-violence. It includes the ability to anticipate a desirable future while working to avoid undesirable scenarios. The approach reverses the traditional paradigm, which holds that we must learn from the past for the sake of the future. Instead, peacebuilders like Sanam take the desired future as the starting point for our actions in the present. Sanam evokes a memorable image for this: peacebuilders do not sit opposite each other (like parties to a conflict engaging in negotiations) but side by side, looking into the future they hope to create together.

Another elementary peacebuilding principle is acknowledging that different people may have different truths about one and the same event. Injuries, harm and suffering must not be relativized; there are moral boundaries, red lines. But this principle describes the willingness to look at a situation or experience from different perspectives.

I experienced the power of this principle during the Colombian peace process. In 2016 I lived in the centre of the capital, Bogotá, for a few months, working in the feminist organization Sisma Mujer. I arrived in Bogotá on 1 October 2016, just one day before the referendum on whether to accept a peace treaty between the government and the left-wing guerrilla movement, FARC.† The peace treaty put before the Colombian people was one of the most inclusive in the history

---

* I devote a whole chapter to this topic in my book *The Future of Foreign Policy Is Feminist*, see pp. 117–48.

† Fuerzas Armadas Revolucionarias de Colombia – Ejército del Pueblo (Revolutionary Armed Forces of Colombia – People's Army).

of the world, and Sisma Mujer had made a major contribution to it. Unfortunately the population voted to reject the treaty, albeit by a very narrow margin.*

When the revised treaty was signed by the government and FARC on 24 November 2016 (this time without a referendum), it was of historical importance, despite the antifeminist attacks that had been aimed at it. Among other things, it was the first time in world history that such a treaty had acknowledged the perspectives of women and other political minorities, and the realities of their lives: more than a hundred provisions related to the prevention of gender-specific discrimination. This included, for example, the redistribution of land, which – as in other countries – is mainly owned by men. The treaty also decreed that there must be zero tolerance for sexualized and gender-specific violence. The peace treaty led to one of the most successful disarmament operations in history, with nearly nine thousand weapons surrendered.

Although other governments and various organizations strongly supported the process, it was local feminist civil society that ensured the progressive nature of the peace treaty. The positive outcome is the result of their ability to work together, despite different opinions and perspectives on the same situation.

I soon became aware of this special and deliberately culti-vated ability. A few months after the peace referendum, my boss at Sisma Mujer, who is well known throughout Colombia as a feminist and human rights defender, invited me to a meet-ing one evening in a smart hotel in Bogotá. I was surprised to see security guards with machine guns standing outside the conference room. Until then I hadn't fully realized the danger

---

* The 'no' campaign, led by the former president of Colombia, Álvaro Uribe, won by a margin of just 0.4 per cent, or 54,000 votes. Yet the Colombian civil war, since its beginning in the mid-1960s, had cost more than 220,000 lives and displaced more than six million people.

faced by human rights defenders in Colombia. The room contained only women: leading campaigners for human rights and women's rights, including professors, lawyers, heads of NGOs and representatives of FARC.

The women, some of them arch-enemies, had come together to discuss the practical implementation of the peace treaty and its concessions to women and other socially oppressed groups, such as LGBTQI+ people, Afro-Colombians, or the indigenous population. 'Even if we don't agree on everything, we have to pull together,' said one of the feminists sitting at my table. Although they were on different sides, these women were united by the desire for a more equal society, and they were prepared to accept the perspectives of the 'other' side.

Peacebuilding is not a football match, in which one side wins and the other loses. True peacebuilders are opposed to all those who regard violence – whether in deeds or words – as a viable means of conflict resolution. Anyone working as a peacebuilder will soon find themselves caught between two fronts, attacked from both (or all) sides, because they refuse to be co-opted by any party and instead try to build bridges. This can be painful, but it's also a sign that they're maintaining their own independence and integrity with regard to the core principles of peacebuilding.

Peacebuilding requires a huge amount of responsibility, while leaving you open to attack from all sides. I know this from my own experience: both sides try to discredit or vilify you, or pressure you into taking their side. The greatest challenge, for a person playing a mediating role in such situations, is to keep seeking the humanity in everyone. 'As peacebuilders, all we have is our integrity,' Sanam told me in a 2024 video call. And, she added, solidarity with others who are also committed to the philosophy of peacebuilding.

Sanam has met women who have lost their children to war, gun violence and terrorism. She said: 'When I see how they go through this unimaginable pain and then tell themselves: "This happened to me, but I don't want it to happen to anyone else," then I can only acknowledge this compassion and empathy with humility.' She continued:

> There are people in the world who lose everything. They can choose to be transformed by this, to change their lives in a positive or negative way. And there are those who convert their pain and trauma into positive actions and thus make an extraordinary contribution. I wish everybody understood this.

The work that people like Sanam do internationally can be translated very simply and directly into principles for our everyday life and can help us to become empathetic. Peacebuilders build bridges instead of tearing them down. Even in the most complicated and seemingly hopeless situations, they try hard to find common ground, make peace and save human lives. Their goal is to reach a consensus in situations with seemingly insurmountable disagreements.

If even warring parties are capable of this, then it must also be possible for individuals – or at least for those who feel they share the same basic political position. However, left-wing and feminist* actors have a strong tendency to define themselves by their opposition to things – be it the system, the patriarchy or capitalism – and sometimes they're especially quick to oppose their own comrades-in-arms. This attitude weakens left-wing movements and plays into the hands of right-wing and far-right groups. Susan Neiman has described how the absence (or at least the crumbling) of a united front against the Nazis in the 1930s contributed to their rise. In today's world, marked by

---

* For me, feminism is a collective term for theories and movements which demand and engage in political organization and activism. It is a tool for analysis and calls into question existing power hierarchies. It articulates utopias and visions for an equal and fair society, in which all people can live free of oppression, marginalization and exclusion. According to my understanding, feminism cannot be right-wing.

the global growth of far-right and anti-democratic tendencies, we can't afford to make the same mistakes.[14] So if even parties to conflicts and wars are able to find common ground, then we should also be able to do this within a democratic discourse and between left-wing movements. The British MP Jo Cox, who was murdered in cold blood by a far-right extremist in the lead-up to the Brexit referendum in June 2016, once said: 'We are far more united and have far more in common than that which divides us.' This credo encapsulates the basic conviction of all peacebuilders.

Ultimately, peacebuilding is based on simple principles. Saying 'Yes, and. . .' rather than the restrictive 'Yes, but. . .' is one of them. By adopting positive perspectives, we promote cooperation and openness instead of limitations. This attitude creates a space in which ideas can develop and thrive. This is not about delegitimizing criticism. Constructive criticism is an important prerequisite for developing our positions or ideas in a positive direction.

Another aspect is building trust. The mainstays of trust are loyalty, reliability and consistency. Like a tree, trust takes a long time to grow but can be destroyed very, very quickly. Disrespect can close doors which excuses and apologies cannot reopen. Trust is the key to effective peace work and to any successful political activity.

Peacebuilding also requires us to continually re-examine our own position. If we're unwilling to admit to ourselves that we might be part of the problem, we can never be part of the solution. Sincere listening is needed, not just to answer, but to understand. This means asking questions, not making accusations.

Here's an example. At the end of October 2023, public uproar on social media worldwide reached an alarming climax. Just a few weeks after the brutal attack on Israel by Hamas and the subsequent launch of Israel's destructive military operation, the online political world was split into two camps: Israel or Palestine. Many positioned themselves on either one side or the other. Secondary conflicts broke out all over the world. Thousands of miles from the theatre of war, alliances and friendships were shattered.

A great deal of trust and cooperation, built up over years within movements and organizations and between actors, was destroyed by allegations and mutual incriminations. The progressive feminist community in Berlin was no exception. Any attempt to express empathy and compassion for Jews or Israelis, for example on Instagram, was met with vehement attacks and accusations of abandoning the Palestinians – and that's a diplomatic paraphrase of what was actually said. At the same time, Instagram posts that showed empathy and compassion for Palestine triggered the opposite reaction: the writers were accused of abandoning the Jews. It was an unbearable time on social media.

More and more often, I found myself wondering how such a complex conflict could ever be solved if even here in Germany, far from the war zone, we were at each other's throats. I published the following lines on Instagram:

I'm 'surprised' at how we, parts of some bubble, are talking to each other. Accusing & making assumptions instead of asking questions. I'm surprised by how quick people are to judge. Not knowing the other's reality but judging, accusing, & sending violent DMs. [. . .] Demanding, accusing instead of asking. Not willing to see beyond one's own reality. [. . .] Constructive feedback, criticisms & questions are great. But can we please talk about how we talk to each other? How are we supposed to create lasting peace on a global scale if we don't listen, communicate respectfully and deescalate on a small scale? I'm not talking about the 'what' (the content), but the 'how', how we communicate with each other. Can we please be respectful when we talk to each other? Someone recently said this: 'If our own community does not see how it is part of the problem it cannot be part of the solution.' Of course we can continue to treat each other this way, but then not much will be left than the (far) right, which they'll be happy about.[15]

Months after writing these lines, I read an echo of my words in a text by Lena Gorelik, Miryam Schellbach and Mirjam Zadoff, in their important anthology *Trotzdem sprechen* (Speaking nonetheless): 'These proxy debates are reaching a previously unknown note of finality. This makes it impossible to try to carry on the conversation – as we urgently need to do – despite differences of opinion: a conversation that involves listening, the desire to understand, or at least a willingness to tolerate the other position.'[16] The often expressed wish for lasting worldwide peace will only become a reality if we apply the principles of peacebuilding in private, in our interaction and communication with others. These principles do not define *what* we fight for, but *how* we set out upon this path.

# 3

# Resistance

My bookcase is the heart of my home. Eight shelves high, reaching from floor to ceiling, it is full of books, arranged by colour and sorted into favourites and literary masterpieces.

I have a particularly large collection of books on the subject of resistance, and especially resistance by women: the courageous, rebellious women of Iran; the four Mirabal sisters, who opposed the dictatorship of Rafael Trujillo in the Dominican Republic; *How to Start a Revolution* by Pussy Riot artist Nadya Tolokonnikova. The books tell the story of Latin American feminism, and especially of the Argentine feminists fighting against the church and the patriarchy. They tell of Anita Augspurg and Lida Gustava Heymann and the other feminists and pacifists who rebelled against militarization and the state in early twentieth-century Germany. My bookcase houses the history of the women in Belarus who rose up with Sviatlana Tsikhanouskaya against dictator Alexander Lukashenko. The collection includes the autobiography of Filipino Nobel Peace Prize laureate Maria Ressa, *How to Stand Up to a Dictator*, and books about Afghan women resisting the Taliban. One book tells how the Liberian Nobel Peace Prize winner Leymah Gbowee fought for peace in her country. Works by or about Gloria Steinem, Frida Kahlo, Hannah Arendt, Simone de Beauvoir, Maya Angelou, Margaret Atwood, Toni Morrison, the Guerrilla Girls and many other rebellious women have a firm place in the sanctum of my personal library.

Every single day, my book collection reminds me of the importance of protest and resistance. In a famous letter written from his prison cell in Birmingham, Alabama, Martin Luther King wrote: 'History is the long and tragic story of the fact that privileged groups seldom give up their privileges voluntarily.'[1] This is why protest and resistance are so crucial for the development of a fairer and less violent society.

But women who resist and rebel do not fit into the patriarchal narrative of our society. The German journalist and political scientist Antje Schrupp wrote an Instagram post about the traditional division of roles into professional female mourners (*Klageweiber*) and male warriors (*Kriegsmänner*). The women 'have the function of taking care of the unbearable grief and compassion for the victims, without regard for political differences'. This outsourcing of grief allows the men to 'conduct their violent business without empathy and compassion'.[2] It must be clear from the gendered division of labour that this is not about women having the 'good' role and men the 'bad' role, Schrupp adds. Rather, the two parts stabilize each other, and the 'unpolitical' mourning women become a core component of the overall concept.

What Schrupp describes here corresponds to the typical roles allocated to men and women in patriarchal societies, which distinguish between male use of force and female caring, including compassion for victims. The traditional gender roles make women responsible for empathy and men for resistance, which is often associated with violent action. Two examples confirm this. First, a photo in the German Resistance Memorial Centre in Berlin shows nearly exclusively men. Second, books on the topic of resistance are rarely written by or about women. My bookcase is certainly not representative in this respect. But it shows how important this resistance – in both major and minor matters – is for the feminist movement, as well as for my own attitude. And it shows that resistance can be non-violent.

Crime statistics confirm that women are not associated with violence: men are ten times more likely to to commit violent crimes (in all countries). The US psychologist David P. Barash puts it very succinctly: 'The overwhelming maleness of violence is so pervasive in every human society that it is typically not even recognized as such; it is the ocean in which we swim.'[3] Worldwide, almost all violent crimes are committed by men. But this doesn't mean that women are only capable of empathy and compassion, and not of rebellion. If, instead of choosing *either* empathy *or* resistance, we opt to combine the two, this is the ideal path to truly sustainable positive change – whether social, cultural, or political.

Of course women are capable of resistance. The best example of this is the feminist movement, which has been resisting the patriarchal world order for more than two hundred years. Yet, despite all the small-scale progress that has been made, the patriarchy continues (without justification) to place men at the head of states, institutions and families. Men hold sway in the public sphere, while women and other marginalized groups are pushed aside into the private sphere.

If women break out of the private sphere, they are punished with (often very subtle) forms of violence, from the repression of the British suffragettes fighting for the right to vote to today's widespread digital violence against women who publicly campaign for feminism and equal rights.

When women put up resistance, they usually do so without violence. Over the decades (and the centuries), feminists have almost completely eschewed extreme forms of physical violence in their struggle to achieve a just society for all.* If women

---

* Although pacifism is a major cornerstone of feminism, feminists are not intrinsically peaceful and non-violent. When I write that feminists (have)

do become violent, they often have different reasons from men. In *The Furies* Elizabeth Flock describes, in the words of her subtitle, *Three Women and Their Violent Fight for Justice*. She quotes the author Nimmi Gowrinathan and her book *Radicalizing Her: Why Women Choose Violence*: if a woman resorts to using a weapon, it is because she herself is a target.[4]

A society that wishes to overcome violent, patriarchal structures must first overcome the binary thinking that equates men with resistance and women with empathy. Feminist action therefore means becoming politically active, analysing and questioning power relations, but at the same time retaining our capacity for empathy and compassion. We must be capable of feeling human suffering, including that of those who are outside our in-group, while resisting the structures that cause this suffering.

I want to encourage women to break out of the helplessness and invisibility within which patriarchy has historically imprisoned us (and where it still tries to keep us) and play a constructive part in shaping society. Men can also benefit from the disruption of patriarchal logic, gaining a wider range of life choices. Empathy and care can enrich their lives and can be understood and integrated as instruments for shaping society.

## Sisterhood

Resistance from women has many forms, one of which is sisterhood. Sisterhood encompasses solidarity, friendship, loyalty and mutual support between women, and is often based on

---

change(d) society in a largely non-violent manner, I say this despite my knowledge of the sometimes violent methods of the suffragette movement, and despite my own experience of the violent language used by some self-styled feminists. Nonetheless, it is certainly worth celebrating the fact that feminists, over the last two to three centuries, have succeeded in changing our society without violence.

joint experiences, values or goals. Sisters can be friends, companions along the road, fellow fighters. Sisterhood is about closeness, care and standing up for each other. It's about being sisters in spirit, fighting for a common cause. Sisterhood is especially important in societies where national identities are based on *fraternité* or brotherhood.* Wherever masculinity and brotherhood are considered as the standard, sisterhood is the attempt to disrupt the prevailing patriarchal structures by strengthening the bonds between women. Sisterhood is care and resistance rolled into one.

For centuries, girls and women were brought up to consider other women as rivals – competing in looks, competing for male attention, and later, with advances in equality, competing in the workplace. Cat fights or 'bitch fights' were a well-established component of pop culture during my childhood and youth in the 1990s and 2000s. This image of girls and women who despise each other was perpetuated in many successful teen films and series, such as *American Pie*, *Mean Girls*, *Gossip Girl* and *Clueless*. Much has changed in recent years, especially in pop culture, with stars such as Taylor Swift, Beyoncé, Rihanna and many others standing up for sisterhood.[†] Despite this, internalized misogyny is widespread.

At school, groups of girls stand around gossiping about other girls, and this behaviour often continues in lecture theatres and workplaces. It is a product of the patriarchy: historically speaking, men and marriage were virtually the only way for women to gain financial security and freedom, and this forced them

---

* As in France's motto 'Liberté, égalité, fraternité', or in Germany's national anthem, which contains the lines: 'Einigkeit und Recht und Freiheit / für das deutsche Vaterland! / Danach lasst uns alle streben / brüderlich mit Herz und Hand!' (Unity and justice and freedom / For the German fatherland! / Let us strive for this together, / Brotherly with heart and hand).

† In the 1990s, the only public example of sisterhood available to adolescents like me was the Spice Girls, the first world-famous female pop group to practise sisterhood.

to compete for the available men. And in a patriarchal world, men benefited from this behaviour: when women fight each other instead of acting in solidarity, those in positions of power have nothing to fear. This is a self-sustaining mechanism of the patriarchy, which we can only disrupt with feminist resistance and sisterhood.

My life changed radically once I began to see women not as rivals, but as the impressive personalities that they are. I've met many women who have inspired me, challenged me, and above all supported me. Because strong women help each other up. Today I consider myself very fortunate to know that I have both a close and a wider circle of women around me, women who are changing and shaping society in many different areas and supporting each other as best they can along the way.

I first had this inspiring experience of real, lived sisterhood in 2015, when I was studying at Oxford. I met the Scottish peacebuilder Scilla Elworthy, who lives near Oxford, at a book launch. Scilla had already been nominated an incredible three times for the Nobel Peace Prize. She has founded several organizations which work on nuclear disarmament, local peacebuilding and women's rights. I began to work for her alongside my studies. We're still friends today and see each other regularly, and she has continued to be a mentor for me. At the time, Scilla was in her early seventies and had been working to help other people for decades. She has built up an impressive network of women who are changing our world for the better.

About ten years ago, Scilla said something to me which influenced me strongly and changed my outlook:

> The wars and the injustice in our society are partly caused by the fact that we have been raising women as rivals for centuries. We will only see truly profound changes when something truly extraordinary happens: when women begin to support each other and work together.

Today, years later, living and lived sisterhood with many fantastic women has become my reality. I'm incredibly grateful for this.

When women and feminists are publicly defamed, sisterhood – with its special form of trust, solidarity and loyalty – is a great help. But it's also useful when we go into battle mode and resist. At the beginning of 2024, for example, the German justice minister Marco Buschmann (from the liberal FDP) and the German government were blocking the inclusion of an EU-wide definition of rape in the directive on violence against women.[*] I was furious. Every year an estimated 1.5 million women are raped in the EU. Hardly any of them will ever experience justice and see the perpetrator behind bars. In fourteen EU states, the victim still has to prove that she has defended herself physically against her attacker. There is no such thing as 'Yes means yes' or even 'No means no'. Even in Germany only about 1 per cent of all rapists are convicted.

I wasn't prepared to simply accept the blockade by the justice minister and the government. With the support of the German Women Lawyers Association,[†] I drafted an open letter and designed a campaign that was endorsed and supported by more than 150 prominent women from the worlds of politics, culture and business. I would never have managed all this on my own. The greatest challenge was that it all had to happen very fast. The legal arguments, the social media campaign, the press relations and the preparation of content – all this had to be organized within just a few days.

It was only possible to do this thanks to sisterhood networks that were already in place. I asked Luisa Neubauer, the German face of Fridays For Future, and Düzen Tekkal, a multi-award-winning German human rights defender of Yazidi descent,

---

[*] This directive is the first comprehensive legal instrument at EU level to combat violence against women and domestic violence.
[†] Most notably, Dilken Çelebi and Céline Feldmann.

whether they were willing to be the first signatories, along with me. It was clear that this would mean a lot of public exposure for them. But they trusted me to organize everything professionally and protect them from attacks to the best of my ability. They both said 'yes' while the campaign was still under construction.

Janina Hell, one of the two founders of the feminist network FRAUEN100, played an important role in supporting our work. In 2021 she and her business partner Felicitas Karrer launched what is probably the most powerful women's network in Germany. When it mattered most, Janina provided access to her personal network of prominent women, helping us give the project the high public profile it needed. Thanks to her, we were able to persuade various members of the network to sign the open letter: the author and philosopher Carolin Emcke, the actors Collien Ulmen-Fernandes, Gizem Emre and Maria Furtwängler, the TV presenters Frauke Ludowig and Mareile Höppner, the boxing world champion Regina Halmich, the model and entrepreneur Sara Nuru, the author Tara-Louise Wittwer and over a hundred others – a remarkably diverse range of women from public life. All the major media reported on our demands,[5] and we gave numerous interviews setting out our arguments. This is true sisterhood.

Resistance – to obtain more justice and bring about important social and political changes – works when those who have common goals give each other trust and solidarity. Although the German justice minister maintained his blockade against standardizing the definition of rape at EU level, we did achieve something: he agreed to review the legislation on this topic at national level.* Furthermore, it was the first time that we had organized such a successful, high-profile joint protest by prominent women. This remained relevant in the months that followed, particularly when it came to demands for the

---

* With a view to changing 'No means no' to 'Yes means yes'.

decriminalization of abortion.* In Germany abortion continues to be punishable by law. It is only exempt from prosecution under certain conditions, such as the observation of time limits and statutory counselling. The example shows that women can achieve great things when they pull together. 'We are volcanoes,' the US author Ursula K. Le Guin once said. 'When we women offer our experience as our truth, as human truth, all the maps change. There are new mountains.'[6] This was exactly what I felt on the day of our resistance.


## Deconstructing is important, but constructing is even better

Those who wish to change things for the better need to understand where they themselves stand, and how others look at the world. They will find that their own reality is probably not identical to that of others. The extraordinary Mexican artist Frida Kahlo once said: 'They thought I was a surrealist, but I wasn't. I never painted dreams. I painted my own reality.'[7] A fact can be interpreted in different ways, and the interpretations can vary according to context and perspective.

I came across the following everyday example on the internet, illustrating how the same events can be seen from different perspectives, reflecting people's biases and areas of expertise. A person harvests herbs at midnight when the moon is full, and uses them to make an ointment, which is then sold for its special healing powers. Depending on their worldview and area of expertise, people would evaluate this in very different ways. Scientists would say it was humbug; entrepreneurs and marketing experts would see it as a good business model

---

* For this open letter on the abolition of paragraph 218 of the German Criminal Code, for example: https://centreforfeministforeignpolicy.org/20 24/04/14/entkriminalisieren-von-schwangerschaftsabbruechen/.

for gullible customers; doctors and psychologists might see the product as useful because of its potential to activate and strengthen people's capacity for self-healing. Artists might find it entertaining and interesting; they might even join the harvest, one night when the moon was full, in the hope of inspiration. All these different people interpret and evaluate the procedure – in other words, *deconstruct* it – from different perspectives and with different emphases.

A noteworthy feature of the humanities and social sciences is that they teach the tool of 'deconstruction'. Situations, facts, systems, structures and institutions are broken down, theoretically, into their individual components. In intersectional* feminist circles, this process is the foundation for building a fairer society.

When we deconstruct the patriarchy and its effects, this gives us a clearer view of certain norms and principles that often go unchallenged, enabling us to see that they are not laws of nature but have in fact been constructed. One example is marriage. Deconstruction reveals that marriage as an institution was created to control and gain ownership of women, and that the role models of 'man as provider' and 'woman as caregiver' serve to uphold male hegemony in the state and the family. Deconstruction makes it clear why women have to carry out the majority of unpaid care work, and shows that this restricts their access to career opportunities, political influence, and income and asset building.

---

* Intersectionality is a concept from the social sciences, originally developed by Kimberlé Crenshaw, which aims to understand the mutual influences of different social identities and structures. The concept describes how different forms of discrimination, based on categories such as gender, race, class, sexual orientation, disability and so on, intersect. Experiences of discrimination overlap, and these points of intersection give rise to new forms and qualities of discrimination. The concept serves to create a deeper understanding of the variety of experiences and challenges faced by people in different social contexts. Building on this, it can be used to dismantle discrimination and injustice.

If we deconstruct classism, that is, discrimination on the basis of social origin, we understand why upward social mobility is scarcely possible in Germany, and how the multi-tiered education system supports and perpetuates class-based prejudice and disadvantage.*

\* \* \*

In the middle of the process of writing this book, a German government minister invited me to a special meeting with a small group of women, all of whom play leading roles in society and are committed to feminism and human rights. It was an encouraging and inspiring evening.

One of the women present was a social scientist who teaches at a university and specializes in migration studies. As a group, we discussed how we could increase our solidarity and bring about positive social change. The social scientist said that her discipline had gradually realized something: while it was right and important to teach students deconstruction, to hone their critical and analytical skills, the same effort had not been made to teach them the tools of construction. Many students, she said, were very good at analysing, interpreting, evaluating and deconstructing. This is also what I attempt to do in my work. In *The Future of Foreign Policy Is Feminist*, I deconstruct various things: the 'right' sort of knowledge, reality, the nation-state, a particular doctrine on international relations, the military and militarization, the logic of nuclear deterrence and much more.

But just like the social scientist, I'm convinced that, if we want to work towards a fairer world, deconstruction can only

---

\* Germany's multi-tiered education system tracks children into different school types based on academic performance at an early age, often reinforcing socio-economic disparities rather than mitigating them. Children from privileged backgrounds are more likely to attend higher-tier schools that lead to university, while those from less privileged backgrounds often have limited access to higher education.

be the first step. It must be followed by construction and creation.

To have an impact, we all need something we can work towards; we don't just want to be looking at a pile of deconstructed rubble. The famous Brazilian writer Paulo Coelho is quoted as saying: 'The world is changed by your example, not by your opinion.' Perhaps not everyone can present possible solutions, build up an influential network, or found their own human rights organization. But everyone can at least give constructive criticism. This includes saying 'Yes, and. . .' rather than 'Yes, but. . .', as I realized when developing my campaign against sexism in *Bild* in 2014. As noted in chapter 1, my open letter to the newspaper's editor at the time, Kai Diekmann, led to a petition with over 60,000 signatures. I led a team of ten volunteers, working to ensure that our demand was heard. If I'd been in Germany rather than the UK at the time, I don't know whether I would have launched and carried through this initiative, as a completely inexperienced activist. I got a lot of 'Yes, but. . .' reactions from Germany at the time. *Yes*, nice idea, *but* the women appearing topless on the front page of *Bild* choose to do so. *Yes*, interesting, *but* we have bigger problems. *Yes*, cool, *but* you're much too inexperienced to take action against *Bild*.

In Oxford I experienced more constructive good will – perhaps because it's an international setting, with many people who want to create and build, and perhaps also thanks to the Anglo-Saxon culture. *Yes*, brilliant idea, *and* maybe you can also talk to established women's rights organizations to make sure you don't overlook any important aspects. *Yes*, great, *and* you could revise the text of the petition slightly to make it more inclusive. *Yes*, fantastic, *and* it would be important to bear in mind that *Bild* is not only sexist, but also racist.

But it's not just from the outside that we're challenged and thwarted in our actions and plans. I often get Instagram messages from young women, telling me that they don't dare to take a stand on feminist issues. They say they're afraid of not doing it perfectly, and then getting into trouble with their own feminist allies, being reprimanded or vilified. If this is the impression we give others within the same movement, then we're doing something fundamentally wrong. We're not setting an example of sisterhood, but stopping others from getting involved. Apart from the frustration and unnecessary doubts this can cause our fellow fighters, we can't afford this constant 'Yes, but. . .'. Given the huge challenges facing society, we have to get everyone behind us and join forces.

I get the impression that the world is roughly divided into two types of people: those with good will and those without. However valuable and important an idea is, people without good will always focus on the fly in the ointment, and probably assume bad intentions. And yet, to put it in the words of the American psychologist Nir Eyal: 'Kindness is measured by the benefit of the doubt.'[8] I find it hard to comprehend how much effort people put into criticizing 'imperfect' feminism instead of taking action against misogynist systems.

As I was reflecting on productive deconstruction, I thought of the successful German author Benjamin von Stuckrad-Barre. His novel *Noch wach?* (Still awake?), published in 2023, is a sobering example of what happens when people insist on a destructive 'Yes, but. . .' instead of seeing the possibilities of a constructive 'Yes, and. . .'. Although the book is a novel, which tells of 'power structures and the abuse of power, courage and the dark depths of human nature',[9] it was obvious to most readers that this was a fictionalized account of Mathias Döpfner (the CEO of Axel Springer), Julian Reichelt (the former editor of *Bild*), #MeToo and other violations of boundaries. Stuckrad-Barre had been close friends with Döpfner for years and had also worked for his publications. They were so close that the author even became the godfather of one of Döpfner's children. But the two fell out as the scandal over Reichelt's abuse of power unfolded.

The book become a number one bestseller. All the media reported on it, and Stuckrad-Barre appeared on the cover of *Spiegel*. Yet as well as success, the publication met with a great deal of criticism, especially from feminist circles. Well-known feminist authors and activists objected to the fact that a man was being fêted for writing about the scandal. And to add insult to injury, this was a long-standing close confidant of Döpfner, who had benefited from Springer for many years – including generous remuneration for his work.

The backlash was merciless. Stuckrad-Barre and I exchanged thoughts; I felt it was important to support him. I wanted to contribute to a culture of criticism and discussion that was robust enough for a 'Yes, and *at the same time. . .*', a culture that asked questions instead of prejudging. Yes, he got attention and made money with the book. And at the same time, it helped the cause. It helped to expose the conditions at *Bild* and trigger a public debate. Yes, there is structural injustice in our society. A man's word is given more weight than a woman's. That may be true in this case too: almost certainly, the fact that Stuckrad-Barre is a man will have encouraged people to listen to him – more than to the women actually affected by the scandal. This is unfair and wrong, but it's not his fault.

Criticism should target the structures, not those who are opposing them. It can and should demand that Stuckrad-Barre use his privileges to secure more justice. And this is what he did with his book. There's no doubt that male networks have given the author opportunities for access which would remain closed to a woman. What makes his approach rebellious and constructive is that he violated the unwritten rules of the network – after all, he could just have held his tongue. And as a bestselling writer, he could just as easily have written about something else.

At the time, I felt that a substantial proportion of the criticism was unjustified and unproductive. On the one hand, many of the accusations outlined above simply didn't apply to the author. On the other hand, I was concerned on a more abstract level. What if the effect of the criticism was to make men feel that they shouldn't be working towards a fairer, more feminist society, and that their involvement was generally unwelcome? If we only allow those who are victims of injustice themselves to fight for justice, it will be very difficult to achieve lasting social change.

I therefore sided publicly with the author and stressed that different truths can be valid simultaneously. I said that it was reasonable to ask why Stuckrad-Barre was only turning against Springer now, after so many years, when the publisher had been known for its misogyny all along. I also said that it was legitimate to point out that the author had benefited from his connection with Springer for many years. And I acknowledged that it was important to register discomfort when a male author benefited from such a story – financially and also in terms of attention. It's already unfair enough that men in general have more monetary success than women. All these points are important feminist analyses and insights.

However, constructive criticism is crucial if we are to make progress on issues and form new alliances. We should admit the possibility that people can change and develop, instead of assuming that they can't. We can – and in this case I believe we  should – emphasize that it is praiseworthy and helpful that the author has decided to use his considerable influence to take action against Springer and support women, and not only through the publication of his book.

As feminists, as human beings, we must be capable of tolerating this ambivalence. Similarly, those wishing to join the feminist movement should be met with constructive criticism, but also good will. I wish it were possible to say: 'Oh, you're new. We have a few questions, and at the same time we're glad you're here.' This 'Yes, and. . .' is at the heart of constructive, empathetic resistance.

It's crucial to be against something in order to know what it is that we want to change. But if the world is to truly get better, the second step has to follow. When it comes to resistance, deconstruction is fundamental, but construction is even more essential. Articulating and living a progressive vision, organizing a protest against right-wing extremism, starting a feminist network, founding an organization for participation and diversity, writing a thesis that points the way to a better future – all these are examples of the second step, construction. But constructive criticism, which doesn't just seek to knock down and destroy, but shows a way to a fairer future, is also a form of construction. And that's something we can all start doing straight away.

## Non-ideological action

An ideology is a system made up of very stable beliefs, values and principles, which shapes our individual view of the world, society, politics or the economy. People who are motivated by ideology stick to their views and their well-rehearsed narratives and base their actions on these. We all have (and need) our principles. But if someone is ruled by ideology, there is no room for movement and debate. A person whose thinking and actions are based on ideology will be resistant to persuasion by better arguments, reluctant to make compromises and quick to start quarrels with others.

This means that if we want to stand up for a fairer and less violent society, the key is to take a non-ideological approach. Otherwise there's a danger that one ideology will simply be replaced by another.

Like other social sciences, political science avoids talking about 'truth'. It emphasizes that all of us only see a segment of the world, and always observe reality from a particular standpoint. We then try to interpret reality on this basis. Despite all our differences in perspective, it should be possible to at least get somewhere near a truth accepted by all, a truth that I and the person I'm talking to, my peer group and ideally the world as a global community can live with.* When we form an opinion, we should always remain open to the possibility that our conclusions are not necessarily correct, and be prepared to be persuaded by a more convincing argument.

In *Die Illusion der Vernunft: Warum wir von unseren Überzeugungen nicht zu überzeugt sein sollten* (The illusion of reason: why we shouldn't be too convinced by our convictions), the neuroscientist and psychiatrist Philipp Sterzer explains that our own attitudes are often less rational than we think. Our brain constructs worlds that seem right and rational to us. Yet our perception can be a fantasy, which sometimes coincides with the real world and sometimes doesn't. It's important not to let the subjective certainty offered by convictions mislead us into seeing them as the only truths. Convictions should be seen as hypotheses which are open to being disproven.

As soon as people are no longer open to having their ideas disproven, conviction is succeeded by ideological rigidity. This gives rise to an – apparent – dilemma: on the one hand, as Sterzer argues, beliefs that do not have a certain degree of firmness are not worth much. On the other hand, if everyone were to cling unswervingly to their principles, then humankind would have to collectively declare itself insane.

As Sterzer sees it, the dilemma can only be resolved if we learn to understand that unwavering commitment to our convictions is ultimately counterproductive for coexistence with others. Only then will we have the freedom to combat these tendencies. We can and should make an active decision to continually question and review our beliefs.[10]

---

* Except for those who are ruled by ideology or subscribe to conspiracy theories.

How might this work in practice? Mirna Funk gives some idea of this in her book *Von Juden lernen* (Learning from Jews).[11] Here she focuses on the Jewish concept of *machloket*. The literal translation of *machloket* is 'disagreement', and it stands for a typical form of disputation. Funk sees *machloket* as a method for exploring different perspectives and examining the truth in more depth. Her interpretation of the term as a way of thinking coincides with what I've been trying to practise in my intellectual arguments for years: that is, to tolerate several truths simultaneously and to deliberately encounter opposing opinions on the same matter. Through this inner deliberation, this oscillation between different views, I try to come closer to an idea of the truth – only to move away from it again the next moment.

There is no single truth. Coping with the simultaneity of different truths demands ambiguity tolerance. A successful intellectual dispute, in which different positions meet, can help us to get closer to 'the' truth, because both sides allow themselves to move away from their own position and be drawn towards the opposite position. Two opposing positions can coexist, both can contain some element of 'truth' or 'rightness', and, as Funk writes, 'the only chance of truth is to engage in a constant, never-ending movement between these two poles and, through this constant movement, to get as close as possible to the truth'.[12]

A good, productive dispute is like a dance, in which the partners are equal and both are open to leading and being led. And so the dancers twirl across the dance floor, from left to right, from back to front and back again. Dialogue and openness to one another produce the best position. As Funk argues: 'Anyone who claims to have exclusive rights to the truth; anyone who believes that they've understood the world; anyone who claims that others should follow them because they are the grail of wisdom and truth should be avoided at all costs.'[13]

The same goes for the internal *machloket*. Funk believes that we only come closer to the truth if we can unite two opposing positions within ourselves without being torn apart. This tolerance of opposing positions, she continues, leads to a truly productive dialogue between two speakers or between the two (or more) voices within ourselves. It also impedes ideological thinking. This, Funk warns, is

> a way of thinking that we are increasingly confronted with in the Western world at present. Many people are completely incapable of even accepting the existence of positions other than their own, let alone thinking them. Dichotomies are created between the self and the other, enabling people to present themselves as morally superior and others as morally inferior.[14]

On top of this, the incapacity for dialogue – internal *machloket* – and the lack of an internal critical faculty prevent real moral integrity. Conversely, the capacity for dialogue can prevent social injustices and hardships. As Funk writes: 'We need to draw a line under the obsessive desire to be morally superior, always and everywhere; instead we need to turn towards true moral integrity which, knowing its own fallibility, automatically distances itself from moral superiority.'[15]

In January 2024 investigative journalists from the Berlin-based non-profit media house Correctiv revealed that extreme right-wing actors, including the AfD, were fantasizing about (and planning) the mass deportation of immigrants. These revelations were followed by weeks of protests against right-wing extremism in German cities. Such protests are crucial for the resilience of our democracy. They are an important tool in the public fight against fascism and right-wing extremism, and create a strong sense of community among protesters.

After the demonstrations, however, the protesters were criticized on social media by some left-wing accounts and opinion leaders. It was argued that the mainly white people who had taken to the streets against the AfD but had not done the same for Palestine could not be trusted. The sincerity of their commitment was called into question because they had demonstrated for one cause but not the other. I felt that these statements were short-sighted, divisive, ideological and dogmatic – and therefore a threat to democracy. People who were standing up for this form of society were being defamed and potentially discouraged. Such accusations and hostilities drive people apart, at a time when we so desperately need a strong, cohesive movement against the right. My hope was that the anti-AfD protesters would not let themselves be influenced by these criticisms. Resistance against the right is more urgently needed than ever, and it has to come from the whole spectrum of the democratic centre. If we only demonstrated with those who shared our exact views on every political issue, we'd soon be marching on our own.

I do accept that a debate about the accusations from the left is justified, even if I disagree with the accusatory and divisive nature of the communication. It's legitimate and important to ask why there are not more people in Germany protesting against the massive, destructive, military force being used to displace and kill people in Gaza. It's also reasonable to ask why people in Germany are protesting against far-right groups but not against Netanyahu's far-right government. Yet claiming that white anti-AfD demonstrators can't be trusted because they aren't participating in other protests is not only whataboutism, but an ideological approach that only tolerates one specific set of beliefs.

There are many reasons why people take to the streets against the AfD but not against Netanyahu's government. Some of them strike me as reasonable, others not. People tend to pay more attention to issues in their immediate vicinity, with relevance for their own lives. This is important and understandable for reasons of mental health. People have individual priorities, and we should understand and accept this. I personally have been using my social media activities for months to draw attention to the unspeakable suffering of the Palestinians, especially the women and children who are being killed in this conflict. Nothing can ever justify the massive force being used against civilians in the Gaza Strip, in violation of international law. It is hell on earth. Killing was never a solution. What is happening there is inexcusable. It reminds me of Desmond Tutu's often-quoted words: 'If you are neutral in situations of injustice, you have chosen the side of the oppressor.'

And yet we should – and I try to do this every day – avoid black-and-white thinking and allow shades of grey. We need constructive openness, without prejudices, and we need to build bridges instead of walls. Only then can we progress along the path of non-ideological action. This attitude demands a free spirit and a willingness to let go of entrenched patterns of thought. 'Having a free mind in [Hannah] Arendt's sense means turning away from dogma, political certainties, theoretical comfort zones and satisfying ideologies', writes Lyndsey Stonebridge, scholar of literature and professor of humanities and human rights. 'It means learning instead to cultivate the art of staying true to the hazards, vulnerabilities, mysteries and perplexities of reality because, ultimately, that is our best chance of remaining human.'[16]

I wish and hope that other people will take an interest in human rights violations and will raise their voices against them. I do my best to counteract indifference within my sphere of activity and influence, while balancing my own internal attention economy. But defining this for other people is neither my prerogative nor anyone else's; if I were to do so, I would be claiming moral superiority. To build up a non-ideological attitude and defend this, even in the face of adversity, requires not just an acknowledgement that our beliefs are disprovable, but also firm and unshakeable principles. These could be universal human rights, for example, or the unwavering resolve to see humanity in everyone.

## The activist's dilemma

On 8 March 2017, International Women's Day, I was living in New York and working for the United Nations. At the same time, I was writing more and more texts for different media to share my feminist ideas. On this particular day, I'd published an article entitled: 'Neun Tipps für angehende Aktivist*innen' (Nine tips for budding activists). I wanted to share my activist experiences with a wider audience. The first of the nine tips referred to what Friedemann Karig would describe a few years later as the 'activist's dilemma': 'You make yourself unpopular, at least in the short term, to convince people of a cause.'[17] My tip for activists was as follows:

> Abandon the natural aspiration to be liked by everyone. If you want to fight for a society in which, for example, women are respected as much as men, you're going to have to shake some very solid structures. These structures have existed for centuries, they're consolidated by our everyday actions, and many, many people benefit from them. Those that have the privilege of living a life free of discrimination. Your criticism of these structures can provoke aggressive defensive behaviour in such people if they feel they're under attack. So you won't only be making friends. But this is how activism works: it is those who call society into question who enable it to grow.[18]

I have experienced this many times over the years. Even if many people would certainly support the fight for women's rights and human rights in theory, the same people can reject it when the time comes for protest and action. Because at the moment of protest there is friction and discomfort, which many people find difficult in the short term, even if they're grateful for the consequences of the protest in the long term. I am convinced that change towards a fairer society is scarcely possible without friction, which inevitably arises when old logics or structures are replaced by new ones. When activists raise sensitive issues, this can be painful, but it is unavoidable if we want to eliminate injustices. Often this discomfort is projected onto the activists who are raising the issues, rather than directed at the people and structures that have caused the injustices.

This change and this societal growth are not equally pleasant for everyone. For example, the majority of Germans are in favour of decriminalizing abortion and abolishing the obligation to undergo counselling before a termination. The fight to achieve this is not an easy one, however, and as activists, we risk making enemies – even among those who will later be grateful for the long-overdue removal of abortion from the criminal code. It really does seem to be a dilemma, but only if we take the opinions of others to heart. This is a particular problem for those who tend to be people pleasers. I'm not a people pleaser: I have no ambition to please everyone, quite apart from the fact that this is neither possible nor desirable. Knowing and articulating my abilities, needs and boundaries is the complete opposite of people pleasing. If this weren't the case, I would have no self-efficacy as an activist. Thus the activist's dilemma is ultimately just a phase in the fight for a fairer society.

## Cynicism as ostensible resistance and intellectual laziness

So far, this chapter on resistance has been about 'Do's'; this section is about a 'Don't': cynicism.

I experience cynicism constantly, especially at events where I'm speaking. If, for example, I express my views about the need for change towards a fairer and less violent society, someone often raises their hand and tells me it's nice that I'm making an effort, but nothing will come of it in the end. The powerful are too powerful, so it's pointless to keep trying. At such moments it seems at first glance that the person talking to me is resisting these 'powerful' people. But this expression of regret, this verbal shrug, is not resistance, it's something else.

Cynicism is an attitude shaped by scepticism and mistrust towards the motives of others, accompanied by pessimism or resignation. Cynical people tend to always see the worst in situations or people; they often make fun of ideals, hopes, or positive efforts. In their view the world is ruled by corruption, selfishness and ignorance, and they see all attempts at doing the right thing as pointless or doomed to failure.

Despite the many global challenges we face, we are all potentially capable of changing the world and we must not become cynical. Cynicism is nothing but intellectual laziness. It requires no commitment. The real art of resistance, when confronted by vast and overwhelming systems such as the nuclear arms industry, is not to be intimidated by their superior strength but to find specific weaknesses and target these. This is what the Nobel Prize-winning activists of the International Campaign to Abolish Nuclear Weapons succeeded in doing when they secured an international agreement banning nuclear weapons. They were motivated by the conviction that mass murderers or nationalists such as Vladimir Putin and Donald Trump should not have the power to kill tens of thousands of people – or more – at the push of a button. These activists also encountered many people who told them: 'Go ahead. But you don't seriously believe that it'll achieve anything. The nuclear states will never give up their weapons.' Nonetheless, their protest was an important step in the long journey towards the elimination of such weapons. Although nearly all* nuclear states still have their weapons, simply accepting this and making no effort to change it is not a forward-looking option. Consciously deciding not to think about this or take any further action is lazy or the result of bad experiences.

---

* Only South Africa and Ukraine have, in the past, given up their nuclear weapons programmes and surrendered weapons.

I'm all too familiar with such defensive reactions from my day-to-day work. It doesn't matter what the topic is, whether it's strengthening women's rights and human rights, global disarmament, or the fight against the climate crisis. You probably have people like this around you too, people who offer up cynical arguments and think everything is pointless. But it's helpful to be able to dismiss this attitude as intellectual laziness. Being constructive, developing a vision and helping to create a liveable future is hard work. But it's the only work that's worthwhile – and it's work that needs to be done on a small scale as well as a large scale.

When people react cynically to a political or social situation, this is not constructive resistance, which could help to improve the situation. Cynicism is destructive; it does not create and it offers no alternatives. Cynicism is cheap and easy. Usually it's well disguised as resistance, yet it could hardly be further from the real work that this requires.

# 4

# The tools for empathy and resistance

To keep the dance of empathy and resistance in equilibrium, to ensure that the combination of these two elements can help us move towards a fairer and less violent society, we need certain tools. The most important of these are hope, knowledge and networks.

## Hope

A while ago, when the evil tidings of wars, crises and catastrophes were coming thick and fast, a woman I know said to me: 'When I no longer have any hope, I try to be grateful.' This sentence really resonated with me and was exactly what I needed to hear at the time. Gratitude plays an important role in my life; I'm grateful for my life and the people around me. I'm grateful that there are very few moments when I have no hope. If that weren't the case, I couldn't do my job as an activist or as the director of a human rights organization – and wouldn't want to. I firmly believe that we can only do human rights work and political work if we have hope.

Hope is based on the conviction that progress, that is, positive social change, is possible. This belief in progress is one of the core tenets of a left-wing worldview, along with universalism and the striving for justice. As the philosopher Susan Neiman argues, there is in fact no greater difference between the left and the right than the idea that progress is possible. Right-wing and especially far-right politicians and other actors are united in their glorification of and nostalgia for the past. Those who position themselves on the left, however, live with a focus on the future: according to this worldview, people can work together to bring about real improvements in living conditions for themselves and others.[1] If there is no prospect of progress, politics degenerates into nothing but a continuous power struggle.

A glance into the past makes this clear. Over the centuries, living conditions for large numbers of people have been steadily improved. This fact in itself is enough to give me and many others grounds for hope.

In my first book, *The Future of Foreign Policy Is Feminist*, I frequently refer to other women. I include individual portraits of several and mention the achievements of many others. These are women, mostly feminists, who have had a positive impact on the world before me. I stand on their shoulders – as a feminist, a human rights activist, an author and an entrepreneur. My campaigns, for example the campaign to change German criminal law, would not have been possible if there had not been women in Germany, decades earlier, who fought successfully for female suffrage (1918), for the inclusion of equal rights for women in Germany's constitution (*Grundgesetz*) (1949), or for the criminalization of marital rape (1997). And I would never have been able to work on feminist foreign policy if over a thousand women had not come together at the first Women's Peace Congress in The Hague in 1915 to demand a new, feminist world order. As a political adviser, I would not be as effective without the women who played a crucial role in the creation of the UN convention on women's rights (CEDAW) (1979); the women at the UN's Fourth World Conference on Women in Beijing, who produced a comprehensive plan to promote gender equality and the rights of women (1995); the women who introduced the Women, Peace and Security agenda to the UN Security Council (2000); or the former Swedish minister of foreign affairs, Margot Wallström, who announced Sweden's feminist foreign policy in 2014 – making it the first country ever to have one.

These are the shoulders on which I stand. They symbolize progress, albeit in a world where, globally speaking, women's rights are trampled on; a world where attacks on women's and minority rights are constantly increasing, thanks to authoritarian leaders and far-right actors. The dedication and work of the women mentioned above prepared the ground for our present-day realities. These are realities that were only hopes in the past. Hope generates reality.

The Indian-Canadian writer Rupi Kaur captures her gratitude for the efforts of past women in a wonderful poem, 'Legacy'.[2] I too want to help make the mountain taller to extend the vision of women. As an author, I formulate visions, as an activist, I demand their realization, and as an entrepreneur I use concrete projects to show how they can become possible.

A reviewer appraising my book on feminist foreign policy for the British publisher before it was translated into English described my attitude as pragmatic. She wrote: 'It becomes increasingly clear that Lunz is an idealist, but also a pragmatist.' At first I was taken aback by this description; it didn't sit well with me. But the reviewer was right. This is my approach; this is how I try to make the mountain taller. Even though I can never know whether my visions are really achievable, I continue to act, because: 'Hope is not the same thing as optimism. It is not the conviction that something will turn out well, but the certainty that something makes sense, regardless of how it turns out.'[3] This quote is from Václav Havel, the Czech writer, dissident and statesman. Hope is what drives me and gives my life meaning.

Hope is not simply waiting for things to somehow turn out all right. Having hope is not a state, but an activity, a conscious act. Hope is a political choice. I have hope because, in my personal and political life, I maximize the opportunities to contribute to positive social change. This would not be possible without a continuous learning process, an effective, actively created network, based on trust, and the development and leadership of my organization. These elements give me hope, because I know they can help to bring about the change I want to achieve in society.

I regularly receive appreciative emails and messages, mainly from women, saying that my work gives them hope, especially when I take a stand against powerful men who exploit or misuse their positions and mobilize others for this purpose. The fact that I can help to give others hope is no coincidence. It's the product of a great deal of work, but also of privilege. It's possible because I've been deliberately creating the prerequisites for hope for many years in different areas. I'm sufficiently well educated and well read to be able to contradict influential figures, such as government ministers. I've spent years building up a network of influential women; within a few days I can muster the support of legal experts, actors, former ministers, the CEOs of blue-chip companies, famous politicians and authors. With my organization, CFFP, I've now built up a team and the structural and logistical prerequisites to design and run campaigns.

But just as important are all those who create hope on a small scale by changing something in their own personal sphere. The woman who learned to read in a time or place where this was not the norm for girls. The woman who refused to accept her inferior legal status and fought for her rights. The woman who had the courage to leave her violent husband, defying the expectations of society. Hope is not simply there; people create the conditions and opportunities that enable them to contribute to social change and justice.

My friend Jeannette Gusko – a writer who was until recently the co-director of the investigative journalism newsroom Correctiv – once talked to me about how these opportunities could be maximized. She used the 'panda theory' to explain. The very low global population of pandas is mainly due to the fact that female pandas can only get pregnant on a small number of days every year, and even then with great difficulty. To protect and increase the worldwide panda population, zoos and sanctuaries do a number of things to help female pandas get pregnant. These include investigating and monitoring panda reproduction, artificial insemination, introducing male pandas and providing other stimuli to encourage mating, as well as nutrition and breeding programmes. These are all measures designed to increase the likelihood that a female panda will give birth to baby pandas and thus boost the chances of the species' survival. Hope works in a similar way: for me, hope means creating as many opportunities as possible to increase the likelihood that our society will become more just.

Even if the individual power each one of us has to change things is relatively small, it is still real power. Our day-to-day choices about how to live our lives are active decisions: we choose whether to be for or against things, or somewhere in the middle. If we focus on something, the chance of change grows. Change does not begin with us, nor does it end with us. It is difficult to understand, let alone measure, the precise impact of our actions. The effects of what we do are generally not linear, and there may be a time lag between action and impact. But we must not let ourselves be discouraged by this.

In January 2017, the day after Donald Trump's first inauguration as US president, I was on the Women's March in Washington, DC. Along with millions of other people worldwide, mainly women, we had taken to the streets to stand up for our rights. The slogan 'Pussies united cannot be divided' was heard up and down the route of the Washington pro-test. I was electrified, full of hope. That day, women's marches were taking place on every continent, and millions of voices were chanting feminist demands. It was a tremendous, his-toric event, an example of the resistance that will change our society. True, we didn't manage to thwart Trump's misogynist, inhumane and authoritarian policies over the following four years; we didn't even come close. But that doesn't mean our protest was unsuccessful. First, the worldwide solidarity was incredibly encouraging and helped me and many others to get through Trump's first term in office. Second, we will never be able to trace all the effects the protest had. Perhaps there was a little girl standing among the countless protesters that day, listening to the impressive feminist speakers; perhaps the march and the speeches kindled a fire in her, and one day she'll become the first female president of the United States?

## Knowledge

When I was living in New York in 2017, I didn't have much money. The small salary I earned from my fellowship at the United Nations was just enough to cover my rent – for a room in a shared apartment on Manhattan's Lower East Side. And yet there was one little luxury I wasn't willing to renounce: at least once a week, I went to my favourite New York bookshop, The Strand. Thanks to The Strand, I acquired not only a number of good books, but also a special bag with the following words printed on it: 'A well-read woman is a dangerous creature.' The 'danger' emanating from well-read and educated women had a magical effect on me even then. I was hungry for information about women like Malala Yousafzai, who, in her teens, risked her life for her right to education (and was shot and nearly killed by the Taliban as a result). Today Malala campaigns for girls' right to education worldwide. Or Ruth Bader Ginsburg, the astute former US Supreme Court justice. She combed through countless books and articles and gradually succeeded in making the US legal system less discriminatory towards women. I devoured the words of these intelligent and determined women, whose works now grace my bookshelves. All these women made a name for themselves worldwide because of their sharp intellect, and all had a positive impact on their societies. Such women fascinate and inspire me. They really are dangerous creatures, imperilling the unjust status quo with their rebellious writings.

I hope that my books and other texts will also facilitate new ways of thinking and contribute knowledge that can help to challenge the status quo. So I was particularly pleased to hear how often my book on feminist foreign policy has been described as a standard work, and how many university curricula it has been included in. In the book, I investigate how and why the ideas, thoughts and theories of a minority – white men from Italy, France, the UK, Germany and the US – dominate university courses and the world of knowledge so disproportionately, and why they all lay claim to objectivity, neutrality and interpretative sovereignty.

According to Puerto Rico sociologist Ramón Grosfoguel, the one-dimensionality of today's knowledge – he calls it 'intellectual colonization' – is the result of the four 'epistemicides' of the sixteenth century. The first occurred during the conquest of al-Andalus, when the Jewish and Muslim populations were driven out. The second was when the Spaniards began to colonize indigenous peoples, first in America and then in Asia. The third was the trans-Atlantic slave trade, in which millions of people from the African continent were dehumanized, enslaved and murdered. The fourth was the 'witch hunts', the murder of tens of thousands of mainly European women, who were burnt at the stake. This happened because 'their practices of knowledge could not be controlled by men', according to author Emilia Roig. Women were especially affected by all these erasures of knowledge. In the witch hunts, which extended from the fifteenth century to 1782 (when Anna Göldi became the last woman to be executed as a witch in Switzerland), women made up about three-quarters of the victims. As well as ending women's lives, this massacre deliberately and strategically obliterated woman-specific knowledge, spirituality, intuition and practices.[4]

To this day, women's knowledge and literature is denigrated. In comparison to male authors, they receive less attention and are discussed much less often.[*] The author Nicole Seifert has dedicated a whole book to this misogyny in the literature industry: *Frauen Literatur*.[5]

For my feminist resistance, knowing about women and feminists and having access to their knowledge is essential. This is one of the reasons why my bookshelves are full to overflowing with texts and books by these authors. The things I write today, the political demands I make – all this is possible because rebellious women, long before me, disrupted traditional knowledge and male intellectual hegemony.

One of them is the unknown woman whose picture appeared on a public mural in the capital of Lebanon in 2019. On the wall of a parking lot in Cairo Street, in the popular Hamra district, the artist Diana Al-Halabi had painted a woman in a red dress, sitting on a bench, absorbed in a book. In the background, we see angry men raising their fists and shouting, demanding the woman's attention. She, however, continues to read her book, the Arabic translation of Hannah Arendt's *On Revolution*. This was an outrage for the country's rulers because, in Arendt's words: 'There are no dangerous thoughts,

---

[*] In March 2018 a study at the University of Rostock (http://www.xn--frau enzhlen-r8a.de/) analysed over two thousand reviews from sixty German media outlets (press, radio and television). The study revealed that books by male authors were discussed twice as often and in much more detail than books by female authors. It also found that 75 per cent of the books reviewed by male literary critics were by men.

thinking itself is dangerous.' Lyndsey Stonebridge, who interviewed the artist, adds that 'thinking by women [. . .] is perhaps
especially dangerous; and not least when the subject of their
thoughts is revolution'.[6] Clever, well-read women really are
dangerous creatures.

## Networks

It is difficult to have an impact and to achieve significant
things on one's own. This is why my extensive network of
strong, influential women is so crucial for my resistance to
unjust structures. Networks provide access, dialogue and support, the same things that sisterhood offers in direct, personal
relationships. Networks can give us a wonderful sense of
humanity, warmth and care. They are especially important
among women, because our patriarchal societies have historically ensured that women were transferred to the household
and family of their husband upon marriage, leading to the sys-
tematic destruction of women's networks and care systems. In
many parts of the world, this is still completely normal.

This is why I get annoyed by statements like 'Women aren't
very good at networking'. This isn't true: it's just that women's
networks have more trouble surviving. Another reason for this
is that women simply don't have as much time as men, including time for networking: all over the world, women work more
than men.* This is why networking among women is important
and can be considered a feminist act. Feminist networking
resists patriarchal domination, while giving women the support
they need to advocate and advance their common interests.

One of the most influential women's networks in Germany
is the aforementioned FRAUEN100. It would be difficult to

---

* This is mainly because of unpaid care work, of which women carry out a
disproportionate share worldwide.

find another women's network in Germany that has been so successful in combining highly political and feminist content with media attention and red-carpet razzmatazz. But don't be fooled by the glitz and glamour: the themes of the network include male violence against women; the misogyny of the AfD and the far right; the women's revolution in Iran; and feminist foreign policy. This last topic takes centre stage during the Munich Security Conference, as part of a multi-year collaboration with my organization, CFFP.

The successful, influential women who make up the network include ministers and other politicians, actors, human rights activists and journalists. Much of its activity goes on behind the scenes, such as the mutual support and collaboration between the women affected by the power abuse of former *Bild* editor Julian Reichelt, the collaboration between political figures and journalists in the case of power abuse by Till Lindemann, frontman of the band Rammstein, and the solidarity that many women showed for my campaign against Justice Minister Buschmann.

Yet FRAUEN100 has been subjected to a great deal of criticism from both men and women. It has repeatedly been dismissed as 'pink champagne feminism', or eyed with suspicion simply because the women are photographed in glamorous poses on the red carpet. Does anyone seriously believe that smart dresses and cameras stop women from thinking and engaging in politics? The superfluous comments mask a deliberate strategy on the part of the patriarchal opposition: to dismiss and minimize the importance of women's work. This form of misogyny is as old as patriarchy itself and entirely predictable. For millennia, women have been reduced to their outward appearance, and their achievements have been downplayed. The criticism probably contains an element of anxiety, and rightly so: whenever (influential) women come together in networks, great changes occur.

# 5

# My compass in tempestuous times

In my efforts to balance empathy and resistance and work towards a fairer, less violent society, I've often faced strong headwinds. A few strategies, combined with my knowledge about how structures work, help me to stand firm at these moments.

## Empathy is not a zero-sum game

For me, empathy is a fundamental attitude and should not depend on how close someone is to me and whether there are connections that encourage me to sympathize with them. Yet it seems to me that the debate today, especially on the social networks, is growing harsher and less empathetic, ruthlessly distinguishing between friends and foes: 'You're either with me or against me'; 'You're either on team A or team B'. This is disastrous and creates new divisions at a time when we should be standing shoulder to shoulder.

My childhood in a Bavarian village was a positive experience, not only because of the idyllic rural setting, but also because we grew up without mobile phones and – most importantly – without social media. In her book *Alles und nichts sagen – Vom Zustand der Debatte in der Digitalmoderne* (Saying everything and nothing: on the state of debate in digital modernity), Eva Menasse compares this generation, my generation, to a moth caught in a spiderweb. The moth, she writes, probably thinks it can still see what's going on, even though it can no longer change perspective. But at least it was once able to fly, unlike the later generations, the digital natives, who were born in the spiderweb.[1]

I'm not a digital native. I spent countless childhood days and teenage nights without the distraction of a mobile phone, without having to worry that every embarrassment, every kiss, every episode of drunkenness, every inappropriate comment and every unpleasant experience could be filmed, shared and posted. Today we navigate between the analogue and digital worlds, and this strongly influences the way we treat each other – and often makes our interactions more acrimonious. Digital mass communication unleashes huge quantities of highly concentrated emotions and sends them out around the world to, as Menasse puts it, 'turn politics and society upside-down, including the lives of the few digital hermits who have never owned such a device and have never participated in "social networks".'[2] She adds that no war or other crisis has had as much impact as the digitalization of our society – not even the Covid-19 pandemic.

\* \* \*

At the beginning of 2024, Germany was in turmoil. All over the country, farmers were blocking city centres with their tractors in protest against the government; train services were cancelled because the drivers were on strike; and doctors were taking to the streets to demand less bureaucracy and better pay. The sociologist Heinz Bude saw a new quality to these protests; in his view, more and more people were unwilling to compromise.[3] He argued that people now saw the world in a different way. Eva Menasse had expressed similar views: people's behaviour and their cognitive abilities have changed, as have the foundations of human coexistence and the expectations people have of each other; impatience and hatred have increased.[4] And German society is not exceptional: this development can be observed worldwide.

When this more aggressive type of interaction and communication encounters major conflicts such as international wars, the digital debates take on a new intensity. This is especially true when these conflicts are emotionally and historically salient for our society, as in the case of Russia's war of aggression against Ukraine and the war between the terror organization Hamas and Israel. Responses to the conflict in the Middle East illustrate this: social media platforms have morphed into imaginary football stadiums, where there is no cooperation, only confrontation. People stick to their political bubbles, where they are expected to pick a side and cheer it on, while dehumanizing the 'opponent'. It's us against them.

'But what if the objective is no longer to exchange views but to harden one's own position?' writes Maryam Zaree about the rising tensions over the war in the Middle East. 'What if words are just triggers to test which side of the argument the other person is on? What assumptions are at play when we feel less and less able to trust each other?'[5] And Eva Menasse has observed that the characteristics most likely to earn prestige are (verbal) agility and aggressiveness, and that there is no appreciation for gifted mediators, compromisers and peacemakers on social media.[6]

All too often the special human ability to see, acknowledge and commiserate with the pain of different people and groups, and to empathize with different people and groups simultaneously, is lost, first in digital interactions, then in direct contact as well.

Yet showing empathy for one group does not automatically mean having less empathy for another. This was a crucial insight for me. One day after the attack by Hamas, I wrote a post on Instagram. I said: 'Empathy is not a zero-sum game. Showing empathy for one group does not mean you have less empathy for the other.'[7] I added that the only side we have to pick is that of civilians and human rights for all. The reactions were mainly positive. However, the willingness to acknowledge the pain on both sides quickly gave way to a toxic culture of debate, in which every form of support for one group of victims was instantly shouted down (digitally) by the 'other side'.

In his book *Die dunklen Seiten der Empathie* (The dark sides of empathy), mentioned in chapter 2, Fritz Breithaupt analyses the dangers of partisanship, which prevents us from feeling empathy for both or all sides. Here he describes the following process: a person observes a conflict, spontaneously takes the side of one party or the other (as humans we've been empirically proven to make very hasty judgements, if we're not careful), and subsequently sees the conflict only from that perspective. The person develops empathy, which confirms and reinforces their initial partisanship. The dynamic of partisanship and empathy creates a self-reinforcing cycle.[8]

If we don't want to succumb to the dichotomy of friend and foe or good and evil, and to the myth that empathy for one party means less empathy for the other, we need to break this cycle. Because it can lead to polarization, division and radicalization. We must make a conscious effort to see things from both perspectives and to recognize that empathy is not a zero-sum game.

Reminding myself of this, remembering that empathy towards everyone must be possible, is like training a muscle. Knee-jerk reactions, reflex-based behaviour, make this harder. But behaviour informed by reflection and training facilitates empathy.

## Constructive impatience

In 2018, when Nina Bernarding and I founded our non-profit enterprise, CFFP, in Berlin, we had a clear idea of how we wanted to bring about progressive change. We call our approach 'constructive impatience'.

To start off with, we acknowledge that social change can be brought about by a variety of approaches. These differ in their radicality (drastic or gradual change), their time frame (right now, in a decade, or in the centuries to come), and in the proposed starting point for change (inside or outside institutions).

Constructive impatience is based on the idea that we can already see the better future before us and don't want to be held back in our determination to work 'impatiently' towards that future. At CFFP we've opted for a pragmatic peacebuilding mindset. This means that we not only deconstruct unjust narratives, systems and ideologies, but also articulate a desirable future, construct feminist alternatives, call for their realization, and make decisions in the here and now to bring us steadily closer to this goal. We are aware, though, that our striving for universalism, human rights and intersectional feminism – and our vision of a fairer and more feminist foreign and security policy – can collide with the current realities.

To bridge this divide, we make direct contact with the people and institutions we want to influence. We've been criticized for this again and again. For example, since 2020, we've been present at the Munich Security Conference, which is synonymous with traditional military security policy and has close links to the arms industry. As recently as 2022 the media reported that weapons deals were being negotiated at the conference.[9]

One of our core demands as feminist experts on foreign and security policy is a plausible and pragmatic effort to achieve global demilitarization and disarmament.* And yet we still attend the Munich Security Conference. We believe this is exactly where we need to be to ensure that human rights policies are eventually recognized as security policies.

Others may say that we support problematic structures with our presence. This criticism is based on a different but equally legitimate understanding of change, which I can comprehend and accept. The approaches may differ, but their aims are the same: to combat violent and unjust structures and create a sustainably just society. Although we long for radical change, we acknowledge that progress takes time, and that we have to start by creating the conditions for it. There are short-term, medium-term and long-term perspectives. This is why we maintain our constructive impatience and push for transformation while recognizing the complexity of systemic change.

## Difficult women

Women who publicly stand up for a fairer society will inevitably meet with massive online hatred and digital violence. Since I first went public with feminist demands in 2014, I've experienced this kind of violence on a regular basis. Unfortunately, it's part of my everyday life. Sometimes it becomes more obtrusive, usually when I'm (co-)organizing a campaign; sometimes it's less obvious.

My response to the vilification, insults and threats varies: sometimes I cope better, sometimes worse. In good times, such attacks barely get through to me. Over the years, I've

---

* Pragmatic also means that we think it is right to supply weapons for self-defence in the short term, as in the case of Ukraine. But at the same time we demand greater efforts to develop mid- to long-term solutions for global disarmament and demilitarization, so that wars of aggression and the possession of nuclear weapons are no longer possible.

built up a strong network, which offers me both psychological and legal support, helping me to deflect attacks and deal with the hate. This includes my coach, my lawyers and the non-profit organization HateAid, which provides support and legal representation for the victims of digital violence. Talking to other feminist activists also helps. So does my knowledge about the mechanisms of silencing, the tactics used to muzzle people – especially women – who question the status quo. My network and my knowledge help me to recognize that I'm not hated personally, just as a representative of feminism – and as an independent and successful woman. Patriarchal and misogynist societies despise women and want to keep them in their place, especially if they are forging their own path and succeeding. Unfortunately, the hostility that's directed at me sometimes makes me question humanity. At times, I'm so overwhelmed that I have to retreat into the private sphere for a while to restore my strength.

Yet digital violence is not the only strategy for silencing women in the public arena. In recent years, reproaches such as 'You're asking too much' or 'You're only doing it for publicity' have been a recurring phenomenon. They ultimately serve the same purpose: to distract me from my goals and make me shut up. It's always the same slurs, expressed by different people. Incidentally, they don't come solely from men, but – as in my case – from well-known politicians of both sexes. It's always the same misogynist attempts to deny the legitimacy of women and their concerns.

Tragically, these strategies are all too effective: reality shows that they stop many women from publicly standing up for feminism and women's rights. This is not just a shame, it's a major problem for our democracy. I wish that all the women affected by this knew that the attempts to silence us are just that, no more and no less: strategies specifically designed to maintain the patriarchal status quo. The phrases 'You're asking too much' or 'You're only doing it for publicity' say little to nothing about the woman making the demands, but a great deal about the person saying these things. Women have faced the same accusations every time: the suffragettes who fought for the right to vote; the women in post-war West Germany who insisted on their right to respect in the political sphere; the female politicians who demanded the criminalization of rape in marriage; the representatives of civil society who campaigned for 'No means no' in 2016.

I found it interesting and strangely reassuring to discover that even an icon like the pioneering politician Elisabeth Selbert had to face the same sort of accusations. Selbert was one of the four 'mothers'* (alongside sixty-one 'fathers') of Germany's constitution. We have her to thank for article 3(2), 'Men and women are equal'. Selbert was also told, in 1949, that she was asking too much: 'You can't want to rescind or change the whole of family law, that would mean legal chaos,' warned Friederike Nadig, another woman from the same party, the centre-left SPD.[10]

I certainly don't have the arrogance to put myself in the same league as women like Selbert, whom I see as role models, intellectual heavyweights and icons. But I do admit without any pangs of conscience that it's reassuring to know how these women were (or are) vilified and what obstacles were put in their way because of their work and the demands they made. It puts things in perspective. Often I think something along the lines of: 'If even Selbert had to listen to this sort of thing, then it's not surprising that I'm affected too.'

And suddenly I feel more serene, and I remember a quote attributed to another icon, the behavioural scientist Jane Goodall: 'It actually doesn't take much to be considered a difficult woman. That's why there are so many of us.' So, so many – and thank goodness for that!

---

* The others were Friederike Nadig, Helene Wessel and Helene Weber.

## The significance of utopias

We were sitting in the garden of my German publisher, Ullstein, during Berlin's summer festival. Omri Boehm, the German-Israeli philosopher who wrote *Radikaler Universalismus* (Radical universalism), was on the podium and uttered this wonderful sentence: 'Being an idealist doesn't make me any less of a realist.'[11]

Often people who fight for social change are dismissed as naïve and told that their demands are idealistic and utopian. This happens to me on a regular basis. I find it strange (and rather amusing) that people see the term 'utopian' as a criticism and try to use it against me. The fact is that every social change towards greater justice began life as a utopia, before becoming a reality. All major achievements – from the abolition of the slave trade to women's suffrage and, more recently, gay marriage – were once no more than idealistic, utopian ideas.

My work on feminist foreign policy and CFFP's commitment to demilitarization, arms export controls and disarmament mean that we're often told our demands and visions are utopian. Of course, a lot of it *is* utopian. After all, I see it as my mission to develop and promote fairer visions of the future so that social change can happen. Ultimately, people with utopian ideas are visionaries, who are often well ahead of their time.

By definition, a utopia is something that has not yet been realized. It is a positive, constructive vision of the future. This means that anyone can actively help to make a utopia a reality. If we weren't constantly formulating utopian visions of the future, a future worth working for, there would be no point in campaigning for a fairer society.

## Power and the law

Our legal system is not fair; laws are not neutral; Lady Justice with her blindfold is not impartial. Laws are not laws of nature: they were made by humans, mostly men. As a result, they are 'laws that give men more power and consolidate this power', according to the lawyer and author Asha Hedayati. Laws and jurisprudence reflect our societies with all their inadequacies, injustices and discrimination. So we can't assume that they will bring about fair conditions. Hedayati goes on to write that 'laws are the results of political and societal power relations and their negotiation'. She concludes that if there is no critical engagement with the law, it can become an instrument of domination.[12]

It therefore comes as no great surprise that the presumption of innocence does not apply to everyone equally. While this principle is invoked to protect male suspects (particularly if they are famous), there is no presumption of innocence for women who press charges against their abusers. Often the victim/perpetrator roles are reversed and the women are branded as liars, especially if there is a power disparity because the male suspect is famous and has a multitude of (mainly male) fans on his side. All too often those loudly trumpeting the 'presumption of innocence' are doing so to downplay male violence and protect the offenders, while defaming the female victims and complainants in the same breath. This legitimizes and perpetuates the abuse of power.

In recent years there have been several cases of this kind, on which I have taken a clear, public stance. One example is the abuse of power by Till Lindemann, the singer of the band Rammstein. After the accusations against him had been made public, I was in direct contact – almost from day one – with one of the (female) investigative journalists reporting on the case. In the wake of this contact I was one of the first to call for the band's forthcoming concerts to be cancelled.[13] I discussed the issue with politicians and gave TV and newspaper interviews. From this point on I not only experienced digital violence from Rammstein fans, I also had threatening mail sent to my office. What surprised me more was the constantly repeated monologue emphasizing the presumption of innocence.

But, as I clarified at the time in a column in the German news magazine *Focus*, it is simplistic to argue solely on the basis of the presumption of innocence.[14] Of course, this is a precious component of the rule of law. I have no wish to deny it and I firmly believe that it should be upheld in court. However, I criticize the public debate, in which this principle is applied uncritically, without taking into account the context of a drastically unequal distribution of power. I would like to point out that, in our society, over 90 per cent of all acts of violence are committed by men, and male violence against women is an everyday occurrence.[15]

A legal judgment by a court requires a trial. This cannot happen, however, if abuse or rape is not reported – be it because women fear being branded as liars and treated as criminals, because the police does not treat them with sensitivity, or because the trial is likely to retraumatize them. Far too often the justice system does not return verdicts in favour of the victims of sexualized violence because there are no witnesses to these intimate situations, and it is her word against his. Ninety per cent of rapes in Germany are not reported.[16]

And even if a sexual crime is reported, the case is often closed or the offender acquitted. But just because no judgment has been passed or there is insufficient evidence, that doesn't mean nothing has happened. As long as only 1 per cent of rapists are convicted,[17] Germany is far from being a society in which the legal system provides justice for everyone at all times. The percentage of false accusations of rape is thought to lie in the low single figures, no higher than that for other crimes.[18] And yet people evoke this possibility with monotonous regularity.

Every one of us is free to take up a position and to weigh up the probabilities. Do we concentrate on the false accusations, which make up a tiny percentage of cases, or on the far larger number of rape victims who get no justice? We all have the choice.

Automatically and uncritically ascribing more importance to the small number of false accusations not only ignores the laws of arithmetic, but also instrumentalizes the presumption of innocence for the wrong purpose: the defence of male hegemony. We have to finally stop holding up the patriarchal perspective as the norm.[19]

## The noise out there

A few years ago I still found it very hard to deal with insults and hostilities. I hadn't yet learned how to differentiate between important and legitimate criticism on the one hand and 'criticism' that was unworthy of my attention on the other. I didn't yet know that there were things I could just ignore: for example if someone wasn't willing to treat me as an equal. It also took me a while to understand the difference between criticism and carping. The latter has no constructive value and usually no factual basis.

Over time, a realization took shape which still helps me today: if you have a vision to create a better world, there will always be plenty of people whose initial reaction is frustration or negativity rather than appreciation. Digital modernity has intensified this phenomenon.

I also had to learn to distinguish criticism and carping from projection. Often people are actively angry at me. They're angry about what's happening in the world – wars, massacres, oppression – and they ask me, with great reproach, why I'm not doing certain things, or why I've taken a stance for or against something (as if it were even remotely possible for one person to do all these things or take a stance on all these issues). Projecting this anger at me, as a defence mechanism against feeling overwhelmed by the global situation, is absurd and disrespectful – and it's certainly not criticism.

As an empathetic community, we have to change our behaviour in our social interactions, and we have to do so much more decisively. It has to be clear that people can't just fire off their comments wherever they like, without respect or restraint. The author Brené Brown once put it like this:

> If you are not in the arena getting your ass kicked on occasion, I'm not interested in or open to your feedback. There are a million cheap seats in the world today filled with people who will never be brave with their lives but who will spend every ounce of energy they have hurling advice and judgment at those who dare greatly. Their only contributions are criticism, cynicism, and fearmongering. If you're criticizing from a place where you're not also putting yourself on the line, I'm not interested in what you have to say.[20]

So if the critics meet me as equals and take on just as much responsibility for society as I do, I'm happy to talk to them. As for the others, especially the carpers and complainers who aren't prepared to be 'in the arena', I register their presence, but I disregard their objections.

It was so important for me to learn how to deal with the noise out there without losing my way.

# 6

# Women of empathy and resistance

I believe I can recognize the combination of empathy and resistance in many determined people who are working for progress in society. I'm certainly not the only person guided by this attitude, which can connect people, create trust and build sisterhood. I have selected the following women because I associate these qualities with them. I could have profiled many other women (and men); all over the world, there are people changing our societies for the better. One such woman, for example, is the Argentine politician Marita Perceval. After serving as the Argentine ambassador to the United Nations and as Argentina's special envoy for feminist foreign policy (2023–4), she is now the president of the civil society organization Feminists Without Borders. I found myself sitting next to her at a conference on feminist foreign policy in the Mexican capital in late June 2024. Marita's phone kept lighting up with an endless stream of urgent messages. On that day, the Argentine president, Javier Milei, known among other things for his aggressive and unscrupulous attacks on women's rights, LGBTQI+ rights and human rights, was pressing forward with this agenda. Countless trans people were thrown out of the civil service, the ministry of women's affairs was further dismantled, and provisions for protecting women against violence were weakened. While we listened to her in horror, failing to find the right words of comfort and resilience, she said: 'The only fight you lose is the one you give up.' The women portrayed in this chapter embody Marita's words.

## Ailbhe Smyth: the legalization of abortion in Ireland

I still get tears in my eyes when I see the pictures of women taken on 25 May 2018, under the hashtag #HomeToVote. They show women like my friend Jennifer Cassidy, holding their Irish passports, along with a small sticker that reads 'Together for Yes'. In the background you can see the plane that was taking them back from London to Ireland to vote in an important referendum on women's rights. Another picture shows Oxford alumna Muireann Meehan Speed on the plane, smiling. It was partly due to her and her application for financial support that the Oxford Student Union gave travel grants to Irish students so they could get home for 25 May. Several other British student unions also gave their Irish students financial support to travel home.[1]

This was a historic day for the country, and especially for all Irish women. On that Friday, all citizens were called on to decide whether or not the 'right to life of the unborn' should be removed from the constitution. Abortions had been banned in Ireland for many years: in 1983 the country had enshrined one of the EU's most restrictive abortion laws in its constitution. Even women who had been raped were not allowed an abortion. This crime and its consequence are one of the most degrading experiences a woman can go through: after enduring brutal violence, she is forced to carry and give birth to the child – the product of the crime. The patriarchy and the politicians who wish to uphold it could hardly have devised a crueller law. The legal situation was based on the 'morality' of the Catholic Church, which is highly influential in Ireland. This morality is devoid of humanity and empathy – it is, in essence, the expression of a deeply rooted misogyny.

One consequence of the law was that Irish women who were raped and then terminated the resulting pregnancy could face longer prison sentences than their rapists. The 'Eighth Amendment' to the constitution affirmed the right to life of the unborn child, while promising 'due regard to the equal right to life of the mother'. However, a woman who had an abortion risked up to fourteen years in prison – even after a rape.[2]

Because of this law, an average of twelve women per day travelled from Ireland to Great Britain to undergo abortions. So since 1983 (if not before), thousands of Irish women had travelled overseas for an abortion every year. The costs – several thousands of euros – had to be borne by the women themselves. Women who couldn't afford the journey, the accommodation and the procedure had to resort to hormone medication pur- chased abroad.[*] But since the constitution prohibited taking such medications, these women also risked prosecution.[3] For decades the situation for women was unbearable.[†]

But all this would change after 25 May 2018, thanks to women and feminists like Ailbhe Smyth. Ailbhe and her fellow

---

[*] I wish we lived in a world where *Ejaculate Responsibly* wasn't just the title of a terrific book by the bestselling author Gabrielle Blair (London: Penguin, 2023), but a principle followed by all men. It's time men took responsibility for their sexual behaviour.

[†] Some countries are currently legislating to roll back sexual and reproduc- tive rights. The most prominent example is the US. Since the landmark *Roe v. Wade* ruling was overturned in the summer of 2022, abortion can once again be regulated by individual states. As a consequence, there are four- teen states in which women who have been raped are no longer able to get an abortion, or only with great difficulty. An analysis in January 2024 esti- mated that since the new ruling, nearly 65,000 women were likely to have become pregnant as a result of rape in these states, and that virtually none of them would have been allowed to have an abortion. See Jessica Glenza, 'Nearly 65,000 US rape victims could not get an abortion in their state, analysis shows', *The Guardian*, 25 January 2024.

campaigners made history that day. I myself, as someone who frequently challenges influential defenders of patriarchy, have the greatest respect for Ailbhe and the other activists. They put the Catholic Church – which had previously shaped the country's morality – in its place. Worldwide, the Catholic Church is still one of the strongest defenders of patriarchy.

Ailbhe had been campaigning for access to safe abortion in Ireland since the 1980s. In October 2012 a tragic event boosted her protest against the status quo. Savita Halappanavar, a thirty-one-year-old dentist of Indian descent, died of sepsis in an Irish hospital after her request for an abortion was declined. Savita was seventeen weeks pregnant at the time and had gone to hospital because of severe pains. Although her waters had broken and a miscarriage was inevitable, the medical personnel refused to actively end her pregnancy, arguing that a foetal heartbeat could still be detected. Savita's death could have been prevented. A wave of outrage surged through Irish society. The constitution had yet another dead woman on its conscience.*

Ailbhe and her fellow campaigners founded the Coalition to Repeal the Eighth Amendment, which later became part of the Together for Yes campaign. Over time, the female-led coalition brought together around 120 member organizations. In a country with around 4.5 million inhabitants, this was a notable achievement. In 2012 the initiators devised a five-year strategy, estimating that this was how long it would take. In the end it took six years to finally achieve success: the decriminalization of abortion in Ireland.

The way they achieved this was impressive: they resisted the Catholic Church and patriarchal structures, and at the same time they generated empathy within society for women who

---

* The situation is painfully reminiscent of the intolerable status quo in Poland, where several women have died in recent years after being denied abortions because of the country's extremely restrictive abortion policy.

needed abortions. But they recognized that empathy for both sides was needed. When I talked to Ailbhe about her campaign, she said: 'For five years, we had to put ourselves in the shoes of the people we needed to convince, so we had to find empathy for them.' She added: 'When you're developing a strategy for a campaign, it's important that you manage to build up a connection to the people whose attitude you want to change.'

The death of Savita Halappanavar had aroused a lot of emotions in society, mostly shock and bewilderment. The activists had to consider how they could use these emotions for their cause, what narrative and what messages could lead to their goal. They had to reach hearts and minds – and change them. To ensure their success, they chose the path of empathy. They deliberately avoided the word 'abortion' in their messages. Instead they told members of the Dáil, the Irish parliament, that they had to do something because the law was causing pregnant women to suffer every single day.

The feminists around Ailbhe wanted to find a new tone: people had to be encouraged to really feel the distress of the suffering women and to understand the effects on their health, families and relationships. The activists made this an issue that no one in Ireland could ignore. So if men said they had nothing to say about it, they responded with the campaign slogan: 'A woman you love might need your Yes.' A 'yes' in the referendum was a 'yes' to the decriminalization of abortion. This was about care – about looking after each other and caring about each other as a society. In the debate the real experts were given a voice: not doctors and legal scholars, but women who had had an abortion. 'This allowed us to reach people's hearts,' Ailbhe told me.

The activists brought about a sea change – from condemnation to compassion. 'You may be against abortion, you may condemn it, but that isn't the question. The question is: do you really want to stand in the way when a woman needs one?' In a town in southern Ireland, hundreds of pairs of women's footwear were laid out with the invitation to 'walk in her shoes'. More and more women told their stories – of the dangers they'd faced, their fears, the journey abroad. Empathy became the most important tool: *Can you imagine being in her shoes? – No, I can't, but I don't want to stand in her way.* 'What was needed was conversations, not confrontations,' explained Ailbhe. The aim was to make it clear to everyone that this was something that could affect any pregnant woman, whoever she was and whatever she did.

At the end of our conversation, I asked Ailbhe how she and her fellow campaigners had dealt with the opposition. She told me: 'To a certain extent we ignored them. We didn't start any arguments with the other side. Our task wasn't to win the argument, but to win a referendum – and that's something completely different.'

On 25 May 2018 two-thirds of voters said yes to repealing the Eighth Amendment – and a few months later abortion was finally decriminalized in Ireland, under certain conditions. There's still a lot of fighting to be done to ensure abortion is fully covered by the public health service and free of conditions such as a mandatory waiting period. Nonetheless, this is a historic victory for all women.

## Beatrice Fihn: the path to nuclear disarmament

Swedish lawyer Beatrice Fihn was the executive director of the International Campaign to Abolish Nuclear Weapons (ICAN) until January 2023. For years she and her organization successfully mobilized civil society to work towards demilitarization. In 2017 ICAN received the Nobel Peace Prize for its work towards the Treaty on the Prohibition of Nuclear Weapons, which came into force in January 2021. The treaty prohibits the ratifying states from possessing or using nuclear weapons.

Beatrice and I have known each other for some years; her organizations (both ICAN and her new organization, Lex International, devoted to strengthening international law) have worked with CFFP on many occasions. In February 2024 FRAUEN100 and CFFP held a special event at the Munich Security Conference, the third annual women-only dinner. Beatrice was, of course, an important guest.* The keynote speakers were all deeply impressive women, with one thing in common: their resistance to violent actors and systems. They included the prime minister of Estonia, Kaja Kallas (who has stood up to various bullies, including Vladimir Putin), the Nobel Peace Prize laureate Maria Ressa (who rebelled against the dictatorial Philippine president Rodrigo Duterte), the head of Human Rights Watch, Tirana Hassan (who goes after human rights violators on a daily basis), and Beatrice.

Beatrice dedicated part of her speech to hope. She spoke about how we all sometimes feel like giving up. The strategy she proposed was to imagine the process of progress as surfing. Progress comes in waves. In the intervals between the waves, as the water recedes and a new wave builds, our job is to train and prepare for it. It's a matter of being ready when the new wave comes. And while we wait, we should maintain eye contact with each other. This is the strategy Beatrice herself follows.

Beatrice was one of the people I spoke to while writing this book. As I see it, she is one of the remarkable women who have managed to combine empathy and resistance and make them a central part of her work. In our conversation she evoked the

---

* The *Süddeutsche Zeitung* described the significance of the event as follows: 'The word is that invitations to this evening are now almost more coveted than invitations to the dinner the following evening, hosted annually by Markus Söder [the minister-president of Bavaria] in the Residenz [the former royal palace].' Ulrike Heidenreich, 'Hundert Frauen beim Dinner – und wer kümmert sich um die Kinder?' [A hundred women at a dinner – and who's looking after the children?], *Süddeutsche Zeitung Online*, 17 February 2024.

image of the wave once again. She emphasized that, in the current situation with its many challenges, she does not focus solely on the results of her work. Just being part of the resistance is extraordinarily important for her. 'Whatever happens, I want to be one of the people who try to achieve positive and just change.' She added that every kind of cynicism is harmful: 'I would rather spend my time trying than not trying.'

Beatrice is convinced that empathy is one of the most natural human qualities. Wanting to be there for others, caring about each other, is part of human nature. She believes that maintaining this empathy – and extending it to those who are usually not part of our in-group – is absolutely essential for action in a political context.

For years, Beatrice and her team at ICAN worked with countless organizations and activists in their campaign for a treaty to prohibit nuclear weapons. During this time, empathy for the voices and situations of people affected by nuclear weapons – be it by nuclear tests, reactor accidents, or nuclear attacks – was central to their work. The experiences and demands of the *hibakusha*, the survivors of the atomic bombs dropped on Japan in 1945, were particularly important. In the end, Beatrice argues, nuclear deterrence implies that 'my security is more important than the security of the rest of the world'. Empathy makes it possible to broaden this one-dimensional view, to consider people in other parts of the earth, and to make the world a safer place.

Empathy for these people and their experiences led to resistance against the nuclear arms industry and against the nine states that possess nuclear weapons.* At the same time, Beatrice had to resist the narrative of 'realism' propounded by a substantial proportion of politicians, political scientists

---

* Countries known or assumed to have nuclear weapons are the US, Russia, China, France, the UK, India, Pakistan, North Korea and Israel.

and political commentators.* According to this doctrine, all states should ideally possess nuclear weapons to guarantee their national security (which would be an absolute dystopia).

At present there are at least 150 states which have no nuclear weapons and are not part of a nuclear alliance. (Germany, in contrast, is part of a nuclear alliance *and* has US nuclear warheads stationed on its territory.) All these states have resisted the logic of nuclear deterrence and decided to build their national security on different foundations.

In the course of her work on the Treaty on the Prohibition of Nuclear Weapons, Beatrice occasionally experienced internal conflicts between her empathy and her resistance. This was particularly likely to happen when she was accused of taking too hard a line against the nuclear weapons industry – or against the governments of those states whose attachment to the logic of nuclear deterrence jeopardizes the safety of most of the world's population. When this happened, she had to remind herself of who actually had power and posed a danger to others, and why. Once she'd done this, and compared these actors to those who did not have this kind of power and were asking for safety, the course she had to take became clearer. It's not easy to find the right balance between empathy and resistance as we work to make our society safer and fairer. But Beatrice's example shows that we do not have to attain perfection before we can take action. By following this strategy, she and her team shaped international law and, as mentioned above, earned a Nobel Peace Prize.

---

* I have written about this in detail in chapters 4 and 11 of my book *The Future of Foreign Policy Is Feminist*.

## Düzen Tekkal:
## groundbreaking recognition of a genocide

Düzen Tekkal is a journalist, film director and social entrepreneur of Kurdish-Yazidi descent. She is one of Germany's most outstanding human rights defenders and has received numerous awards, including some of the highest in the country. A few years ago she and her sisters founded the non-profit organization HÁWAR.help 'on the ashes of a genocide'⁴ – that of their own religious community, the Yazidis. In 2014 she filmed a documentary in Iraq: *HÁWAR – A Cry for Help* (the original German subtitle was *Meine Reise in den Genozid*, my journey into genocide). The film thematizes the genocide committed by Islamic State against the Yazidis who lived in northern Iraq, with a particular focus on sexualized and gender-based violence against women. On 3 August 2014 the terrorist militia murdered more than five thousand Yazidis, with the aim of wiping out this millennia-old ethnic and religious community. A further seven thousand women and children were abducted, enslaved – partly for sexual exploitation – or recruited as child soldiers. When speaking at events, Düzen always tells of the profound change in her life that this journey triggered.

It is largely thanks to campaigning by Düzen, her sisters and her organization that the Bundestag, the German parliament, officially recognized the genocide of the Yazidis in January 2023. But the work of HÁWAR.help goes far beyond protecting a religious community. The organization runs women's refuges in Afghanistan, amplifies the Woman, Life, Freedom movement in Iran, and campaigns effectively against anti-semitism and inhumanity.

When I talked to Düzen, she told me that her work for the recognition of the Yazidi genocide was both her greatest success and her greatest pain. She stressed: 'We made sure to show who Yazidis are. This is important – because Yazidis have always been dehumanized.' Motivated by empathy for her family and her people, as well as self-respect, she resisted invisibility. She fought to have the suffering inflicted on the Yazidis acknowledged, not only in Germany but also in the EU and the United Nations in New York.

'My personal secret', she explained, 'is that I believe in what I'm doing. I mean what I say and I say what I mean.' 'The public Düzen and the private Düzen are the same person.' This leads to a high degree of authenticity in her resistance to war crimes and human rights violations. At the same time, her willingness to admit weakness makes her vulnerable – especially when she shows compassion.

Her core sisterhood, consisting of her actual sisters, Tuna, Tezcan, Tuğba and Tülin, not only supports her work for human rights, but is also the source from which she derives strength and energy. The same goes for her 'spiritual sisterhood', her friends and fellow campaigners.

Düzen's resistance, her rebellion, manifested itself from an early age. 'When I was a girl, every time someone told me that something wasn't for girls or women, that it was something men took care of, that triggered me.' This went for both big issues like war and peace and smaller ones like the fruit bowl in her parents' house, which she and her sisters were not allowed to touch if there were men in the room. 'I kept practising this resistance in my Kurdish household, risking family strife every time.' Yet her resistance was not just for herself; it always had a broader scope. 'The process of negotiation was always for the collective – everyone I love has to be OK.'

Today, in the fight for freedom, Düzen enters the public arena as an activist, but then returns to gather up the others, those who are not fighting on the frontline like herself. Her intuitive sense of injustice causes her to resist when her boundaries are transgressed. This happens again and again, as she regularly experiences anti-Kurdish and anti-Yazidi racism.

Her empathy and instinct for rebellion developed in crises and in the experience of exclusion – both in her schooldays and today. 'As a marginalized group within a marginalized group, you never belong to a majority.' This is painful, but also gives strength and resilience.

In an interview at the beginning of 2024 she mentioned how little time she had for 'angry hobby activists', who construct their own relevance from their constant state of rage.

> Nelson Mandela wasn't angry. He said that the moment when he lost compassion for his guards would be a difficult moment. He always retained his humanity, even in prison. A lot of activists today don't understand this. They think it's enough to be outraged about something. It's a huge misunderstanding to believe that activism revolves around the mental state of the activist. Anger can be a motor, but it can also be a nuisance, because it clouds our view.[5]

In conversation with me, she added: 'For me, resistance means: do what you believe in, even if you find yourself facing a headwind. And if you can remain standing despite the headwind, this will strengthen both your empathy muscle and your resilience muscle.' These are the muscles we need to stand up for what we believe in.

## Stellah Bosire:
### advancing health justice and dignity in Kenya

The story I am about to tell – Dr Stellah Bosire's story – is beyond remarkable. In fact, I struggle to find the right words to capture just how extraordinary her life and journey have been.

Stellah Bosire was born and raised in Africa's largest slum, Kibera, in Nairobi, Kenya. She grew up in poverty, spending most of her childhood homeless and on the streets. Her mother suffered from schizophrenia and depression. Stellah is a survivor of prolonged sexual abuse and gang rape. By the age of nine, she had already become addicted to drugs – the same age at which she became engaged in transactional sex to feed her siblings.

This is how Stellah's story began, but it is not what defines her.

Not long ago, I faced one of the biggest crises of my life. At a time when I barely knew Stellah, she picked up the phone and called me. Many in the international feminist movement were aware of what was happening, but few reached out. She did. And she did so with an extraordinary sense of compassion and empathy. 'How are you? Are you eating? How can I support you?' she asked. She listened, she cared, she showed true sisterhood.

What defines Stellah is not just her resilience but also her kindness, her courage, her intellect, and – above all – her deep empathy for others and her unwavering resistance to injustice.

When she was twelve, an elder in her community told her she should die. When I talked to her for this book, she recalled: 'That broke my heart. While there was little joy in my life, there were still moments of kindness. I was privileged to be surrounded by women who treated me with care when my mother was unable to, and I also had teachers who showed me compassion.' When she was expelled from school for the last time, those very teachers stood up for her.

From high school onwards, her story took a turn. It quickly became evident that she was exceptionally bright. In fact, she was offered a full scholarship to study medicine in Italy. However, she chose not to accept it, instead staying in Kenya to care for her mother, whose health was failing. She enrolled at the University of Nairobi, where she completed bachelors' degrees in medicine and surgery. Today, Stellah is a medical doctor, a lawyer, and the CEO of her own organization, the Africa Center for Health Systems and Gender Justice. Stellah is also the chairperson of Amnesty International Kenya.

I first met Stellah not too long ago, at a feminist network gathering in Mexico City in July 2024. She was there incognito, having participated in protests and resistance against the Kenyan government, which led to retaliation against her. From the very beginning, her spirit of resistance and her radiant empathy for her feminist sisters in the room were unmistakable.

When I spoke to her for this book, Stellah explained: 'Resistance arises from a place of oppression.' Her work is deeply tied to health equity, gender reproductive justice, and the struggles of disenfranchised communities. 'Resistance is always anchored in oppression – it is, for example, a response to the discrimination faced by women, girls, persons with disabilities, sex workers, the marginalization of the LGBTQI+ community, and many others whose rights are denied. But true resistance can only emerge from an empathetic lens.'

She went on to argue that feminism is about the ability to transpose oneself into these experiences and bring resistance back to life.

> If we consider the fundamental principle of autonomy, why should consensual choice be denied? Stigmatized and discriminated experiences are often marked by pain, yet empathy has the power to drive us toward understanding them. As someone with privilege, I recognize that the empathy I embody enables me not only to comprehend these struggles but also to advocate for change.

Stellah believes that the feminist movement must be deeply embedded in empathy. 'We often speak about integrity and power structures, yet empathy is frequently left out of the conversation.' When talking to me, she elaborated:

> Every power dynamic inherently involves harm on the other side. When we discuss values like intersectionality but fail to

centre empathy, we overlook a crucial element of resistance. Consider how oppressive regimes operate – through harming communities, spreading disinformation, and instilling fear. As intersectional feminists, we cannot afford to navigate these struggles without an empathetic lens.

Unfortunately, she continued, 'our own standards as feminists do not always meet the ideals we uphold. Too often, we are quick to judge rather than engage.' She questioned why feminists are often the first to throw each other under the bus. 'If there is a problem, we must come together, have difficult conversations, and work through disagreements. We do not have the privilege of discarding one another.'

I wanted to know more about the core principles that guide Stellah's work. Her response was simple: honesty.

Honesty is key to our conversations – we should embrace radical honesty. The feminist space often comes with a lot of pretence, but we have the opportunity to change that. When you founded CFFP, the goal was to disrupt the foreign policy space. Yet there's growing concern about the effectiveness of feminist foreign policy for the African continent. How can we bridge this gap? Who among us is stepping into these spaces and taking responsibility to drive meaningful change? And how can we support those at the Pan-African frontline in disrupting foreign policy from a feminist perspective?

Stellah emphasized that we cannot afford to take a backseat – we must be at the forefront of change, not as individuals, but as a collective force. She went on to say that true disruption isn't about pointing fingers; it's about stepping up together to challenge the status quo.

We need radical honesty, not just about the problems, but about the solutions we can co-create. Disrupting foreign policy, funding structures and power imbalances requires collective leadership, collective power and collective disruption. How do we ensure we are not just critiquing but actively reshaping these spaces?

For her, feminism must be rooted in community and guided by empathy and kindness. Stellah believes that

> we must be willing to call each other out when necessary and hold each other accountable, but always with care and a deep commitment to justice. Feminism should be about building, uplifting, and transforming – never about replicating the very toxic systems we seek to dismantle. Our strength lies in how we challenge with compassion, disrupt with purpose, and lead with collective care.

And then there is wisdom – the kind that is rooted in love, generosity, and deep compassion. When talking to me, Stellah reflected:

> My mother was one of the kindest people I have ever known. Even as she struggled with mental illness, she always put others first. I remember coming home from university after using what little I had to buy her groceries and dry food, only to find a long line of women outside our house – she was giving everything away. I was frustrated, but she looked at me with so much warmth and simply said, 'I have you; none of these women have a Stellah.'

That moment changed Stellah. It made her realize the depth of her privilege – not just in what she had, but in whom she had. It also taught her the power of radical generosity and the responsibility that comes with it. 'My mother's kindness wasn't just an act; it was a way of being, a belief that we exist for one another. And that is what continues to shape me today.'

As someone who has lived on the margins of society, Stellah cannot ignore struggle or turn away from pain. She constantly asks herself: 'What can I do to make things better? How can I be useful?' She listens to other women. She learns from them. 'I never miss an opportunity to grow. In the end, in sixty or seventy years, we will no longer be here.'

And so Stellah leaves us with one final question: 'What is our legacy in this world? What will we leave behind?'


## Gloria Steinem: feminist revolution through storytelling and solidarity

It was all very last minute. But I was lucky.

In January 2017, I moved to New York City to work for the UN Development Programme. My visa had arrived just a day before I wanted to leave, and I moved heaven and earth to get on a flight. After just a few hours of sleep on a friend's couch in Manhattan, I got on a bus to Washington, DC, at 3.30 a.m. It was one of the many buses chartered to carry thousands of people – mainly women – to the historic Women's March, held on the day after Donald Trump's inauguration.

Getting a seat on one of these buses was no easy task: demand far exceeded capacity. I was lucky again: a friend gave me the contact details of Laura, who was involved in the logistics of the march and was helping to organize the buses. Laura also happened to be the assistant of Gloria Steinem – not only one of my greatest idols and role models but also a speaker that day. I listened to her in person, electrified. Standing before the crowd, seemingly as ecstatic as we were, Gloria took the microphone and declared:

> This is the upside of the downside. This is an outpouring of
> energy and true democracy like I have never seen in my very
> long life. [. . .] We are here and around the world for a deep

democracy that says, 'We will not be quiet. We will work for a world in which all countries are connected.'[6]

That moment was unforgettable. But it wasn't the first time I had been captivated by Gloria's intellect, power, empathy and resistance.

When her memoir *My Life on the Road* was published in 2015, I was lucky to be in Oxford for her book presentation, securing a signed copy. Reading it in the early stages of my own feminist awakening – just months after launching my national campaign against the *Bild* newspaper – was one of the most formative literary experiences of my life. It helped shape my journey of trying to make a difference.

Gloria once said, when asked how she would like to be remembered: 'I just think as a good person with a good heart who tried to leave [. . .] the world or my part of [it] [. . .] a little more just and less violent and more kind than it was when I showed up.'[7] I want the same thing. And in no small part, that's because of her.

Looking back, I realize why Gloria, her work, and her writing have had such an immense influence on my life. It's because of how she went about creating change – forcefully, determinedly, with resistance, and yet always with kindness and empathy.

I feel that few figures embody the interplay of empathy and resistance as profoundly as Gloria Steinem. For decades, she has been at the forefront of feminist activism, shaping movements, shifting cultural narratives, and challenging power structures. In interviewing her, I wanted to understand how she sees this relationship – how empathy has informed her resistance, and vice versa.

Gloria has spent much of her life travelling. As a child, she lived on the road with her sister and parents, moving around the US in a car and trailer. In *My Life on the Road*, she reflects:

Taking to the road – by which I mean letting the road take you – changed who I thought I was. The road [. . .] leads us out of denial and into reality, out of theory and into practice, out of caution and into action, out of statistics and into stories – in short, out of our heads and into our hearts.[8]

Born in 1934, Gloria Steinem is a pioneering writer, journalist, lecturer, and feminist organizer, who has been a central figure in the women's rights movement since the 1960s. In her late twenties, she gained widespread attention for going undercover as a Playboy Bunny at Hugh Hefner's New York club. Her 1963 exposé 'A Bunny's Tale' revealed the exploitation and harassment of female employees, setting the tone for much of her later work. Over the years, she has co-founded numerous feminist organizations, including the Women's Action Alliance, the National Women's Political Caucus, the Women's Media Center, and the Ms. Foundation for Women. In 1972 she co-founded the feminist magazine *Ms*. Her bestselling books and decades of activism have earned her countless awards and honours.

When I first read her memoirs, one sentence struck me so profoundly that I've quoted it repeatedly in speeches and articles: '[O]ne of the simplest paths to deep change is for the less powerful to speak as much as they listen, and for the more powerful to listen as much as they speak.'[9] This sentence embodies empathy: it urges us to turn toward the needs and demands of those with less privilege and power, while at the same time resisting the dominant, unequal structures that dictate whose voices are heard.

When the feminist movement gained momentum in the US in the 1970s, Gloria became one of its leaders. Reflecting on that time, she wrote:

By then, in the late 1970s, the civil rights and anti-Vietnam War movements at home had inspired more change, including

among women who loved and were crucial to those movements, yet were rarely equal within them. They realized the
need for an independent and inclusive feminist movement that
would take on the personal and global politics of gender.

That realization spread rapidly. 'Altogether, a new conscious-
ness was spreading as women met or read about one another
[. . .]. The dry tinder of inequality was everywhere, just waiting
to be set on fire.'[10]

Gloria has lit that fire time and again. Yet, while doing so,
she has always trusted that '[t]he truth is that we can't know
which act in the present will make the most difference in the
future, but we can behave as if everything we do matters'.[11]
For her, the means are the ends. If we want dancing, laugh-
ter, friendship and kindness in the future, we must have them
along the way.[12]

Gloria sees empathy as essential to the fight for social justice.
In *Gloria Steinem: I Know This to Be True*, she speaks about the
gendered nature of empathy, which I alluded to in chapter 3. 'I
often say to women, "Look, the golden rule was great, written
by a smart guy for guys. Do unto others as you would have done
unto you." But women probably need to reverse it. We need to
learn to treat ourselves as well as we treat other people.'[13]

When I interviewed Gloria for this book, I asked her about
the role of empathy in activism and, specifically, in the feminist movement. Her response was: 'Empathy is necessary in
all social justice movements [. . .]. Empathy actually generates
oxytocin, which allows us to know, care about, or identify with
the needs of the human beings around us.'[14]

When I asked her to share an example from her activist
work that illustrates this connection, she pointed to an early
challenge within the feminist movement.

In the very early days of the women's movement, there were
some white women who wanted to join men in power but not

to join with women of color, who of course needed to contend with both sexism and racism. But it gradually became clear that sexism and racism were intertwined and cannot be rooted out separately.

Her words reflect an important lesson: resistance, if not deeply rooted in empathy, can become exclusionary, even complicit in the very systems it seeks to dismantle. The feminist struggle cannot be reduced to a single-issue fight; it must recognize and address the ways in which different forms of oppression are interconnected. Without that understanding – without that *empathy* – even well-intentioned resistance risks reinforcing the hierarchies it aims to overthrow.

Beyond dismantling unjust systems, I believe activism must also be about building something better. Too often, particularly in online activism, energy is disproportionately focused on deconstruction rather than construction. I asked Gloria how she sees this dynamic. 'Yes, I agree,' she said. 'You can't replace something with nothing. For one thing, we are social creatures and we need to gather together, whether in families or in the workplace. Without some idea of a new alternative, we are likely to maintain the associations we have, even if they are unjust and painful.' Her response underscored an urgent reality: people do not abandon harmful systems unless they see a viable alternative. Activism cannot be sustained on rejection alone. It must also offer vision, a path forward that invites people in, rather than leaving them in the ruins of what has been torn down.

A key challenge in any movement is avoiding the trap of ideological rigidity, by staying open to better arguments, resisting black-and-white thinking, and adapting our strategies when necessary. I see this same openness in Gloria's work and asked her how she has managed to maintain it. 'Each one of us is a unique miracle who could never happen before and could never happen again,' she said.

The movement and organizations we form need to reflect that. It's the main purpose of democracy to allow each person to be unique and to exercise shared rights. One simple rule is to try to listen as much as we talk – and vice versa! Another is to make sure decision-making groups look like the groups who will be experiencing the results of those decisions.

Her response was a reminder of what true democracy should be: not a rigid, dogmatic structure, but an evolving and inclusive process. Listening is not just an act of generosity; it is a strategic necessity. Without it, movements risk becoming echo chambers, failing to represent the people they claim to serve.

I asked Gloria about the guiding values that have driven her work, mentioning the core principles that shape my own work: sisterhood, humanity, constructive impatience, utopian thinking, and the idea that empathy is not a zero-sum game. She responded warmly: 'I love and support your principles! I would only add that activist groups need to look like the people who need and will experience the actions that result. Study, hope, and theory are great – they raise new possibilities – but there is nothing like representative gatherings to assess the results.' Once again, she brought the conversation back to the fundamental importance of representation. It is not enough to analyse and debate injustice; those most affected by it must be at the centre of shaping the solutions.

Gloria's responses also show that resistance and empathy are not just complementary; they are inseparable. Resistance without empathy is hollow, easily co-opted by those seeking power rather than justice. But empathy without resistance is equally insufficient, and risks becoming divisive. The challenge of activism is to maintain both: to understand the world as it is and to fight for the world as it should be.

For me, the most memorable phrase from the interview was: 'You can't replace something with nothing.' That is the work we are called to do – not just to critique, but to build. Not just to resist, but to imagine. And not just to fight, but to create.

# 7

# Why empathy and resistance are so important now

In early 2015, while I was studying in Oxford, I was invited to a lunch in a well-known restaurant in Berlin and flown in from London for the occasion. The guests were fifteen or so prominent women from the German media landscape: editors-in-chief, journalists, publishers – and then me. During the initial small talk before we took our seats at the long table, I got the impression that all the other women knew each other already. I, on the other hand, had never met any of them before, including the hosts, a famous actor and a well-known tabloid journalist. The purpose of the meeting was to talk about how women were represented in the media. The reason I'd been invited was my campaign against sexism in the *Bild* newspaper, launched a few weeks earlier.

In the discussion during the meal, the majority of the women present seemed to think that action was still needed, especially when it came to the representation of women in positions of leadership, but that the situation was largely satisfactory. At least one of them had a leading position at the media outlet I was campaigning against. Since I didn't know anyone and had seldom sat at a table with such an impressive group of women, I was slightly intimidated. But I felt it was important to express my thoughts. I talked about the link between the widespread objectification of women, especially in the tabloid press, and the exorbitant rates of male violence against women. My statements provoked dissent and friction. This felt awkward at the time, but it didn't stop me from expressing my views. I had to say what I thought, even if it put me in an isolated position.

A few days after this lunch, when I was back in Oxford, I had a phone conversation with the actor who had hosted the event (who has, in the meantime, campaigned for women's rights for many years, with a special focus on the representation of women in the media). She said at the time: 'I didn't expect you to take such a definite stance. You looked so innocent and well-behaved in your black dress, with your pink blazer and your long blonde hair. And you were so nice too, so warm and attentive.' She couldn't reconcile my attitude and my clear words with my friendly demeanour. The latter no doubt had to do with the British politeness I was surrounded with at the time, which still has a strong influence on me. 'Don't misunderstand me,' she said. 'I thought what you said was very good and important. I was just surprised by your plain speaking.' Now it was my turn to be surprised: why should the one exclude the other?

Kindness – that combination of benevolence, friendliness and goodness – has played a very important role in my life. Kindness is the yardstick for my behaviour towards others, and I expect to be treated the same way. I'm lucky to have been brought up like this and to have had this attitude instilled in me as a value. At the same time, I've never seen a conflict between kindness and standing up for my values, and for the way I want to shape interactions and relationships with others. In fact it's only become clear to me in recent years, through social media, that there are a lot of people for whom being kind and simultaneously setting boundaries doesn't seem so natural. I keep noticing 'empowering' posts on Instagram which repeat this like a mantra: it *is* possible to be nice and friendly while setting boundaries and standing up for oneself and one's values. Fortunately, I've never had a problem with this.

Ultimately, this is exactly what this book is about: in private and for my own identity, I talk about kindness and boundaries; for my political work, I talk about empathy and resistance. Even though coping with the simultaneity of the two things hasn't been such a challenge for me, it has taken me a long time to work out exactly where and when to draw my boundary between empathy and resistance in the political arena. Whether it's in interactions with friends or romantic partners, or in relation to international conflicts or the best way to change societies for the better, where we draw the line between empathy and resistance is individual and highly subjective. What I wanted to do in this book was to draw attention to this balancing act and give some pointers to help reconcile the two extremes.

Whenever I feel uncertain and don't quite know what stance to take (and, by the way, it's fine not to have an opinion on certain subjects), I take my cue from the people who have, in my view, one of the hardest jobs in the world: peacebuilders. These are people who don't take a side or espouse an ideology, but who accept ambiguities and attempt to build bridges.

*    *    *

Since 2018, when I began working on feminism and foreign policy, and carrying out related projects with my organization, the people who've had the biggest impact on my position have always been peacebuilders with personal experience of injustice and traumatic violence. People who, despite the terrible things that have happened to them, communicate and live humanely, constructively and without violence.

Two such people are Robi Damelin and Ali Abu Awwad, whose work I heard about in the months after the attacks of 7 October 2023. Robi Damelin, a Jewish activist, and Ali Abu

Awwad, a former Palestinian revolutionary, have both experienced tragic losses in the Israeli–Palestinian conflict.

Robi Damelin's son David was killed by a Palestinian sniper near the Ofra checkpoint in 2002, at the age of twenty-eight. After this painful loss, she became the speaker of the Parents Circle – Families Forum (PCFF). This Israeli–Palestinian organization brings together around six hundred families, all of whom have lost a family member in this prolonged conflict.

Ali Abu Awwad's brother Youssef was shot dead by an Israeli soldier at the age of thirty-two.

Despite these personal tragedies, Damelin and Awwad work together for peace in the Middle East. Awwad emphasizes the importance of a peace process that begins with behaviour, and not with a dispute over identities. He stresses that occupation and violence are behaviours, and that real change can only be achieved if people are encouraged to change their behaviour for the better instead of focusing on their identities as Palestinians, Jews, and so on.

Damelin strikes a similar note: 'If you are pro-Palestinian or pro-Israel you are not helping us. You are just feeling good about yourself.'[1] And Awwad says in a podcast: 'If war needs anger, peace needs courage. Reconciliation needs truth.'[2]

To be able to carry out this peace work, peacebuilders like Awwad, Damelin, and all the others need the resources to prepare people and their environment for conciliation and peaceful coexistence. Hatred and pain must be transformed into humanity. This is what grassroots movements seek to achieve with their activism. But it takes more than love and fresh air. Peacebuilders, their movements and organizations need funding.

For me, one of the greatest mysteries of humankind will always be why trillions are spent on deadly weapons and destruction, year after year. In fact, annual spending on arms has been steadily increasing in recent years. We're caught up in a new arms race. Politicians and commentators are falling over each other to demand higher military spending. At first glance this seems understandable, given the increasing worldwide threats posed by real wars of aggression and weapons of mass destruction in the hands of authoritarian strongmen.

But despite these genuine threats, we urgently need to stop militarizing our society and seeing the buildup of the arms industry as a solution. These are just political reactions, not solutions. It is essential to understand the difference between the two. A solution improves the situation, but a reaction is just a response, with no promise of progress.

Whenever I'm contemplating such matters, I like to zoom out a bit and try to look at events in the world from a distance. Again and again, this shows me how incredibly stupid and shortsighted our resource allocation is. Why is so much money spent on more violence, more killing, instead of making a genuine attempt to end this state of affairs and achieve peace?

One of the first sentences I internalized in my role as a non-profit entrepreneur was: what you focus on gets bigger. This applies not only to entrepreneurs, but also to politics. If we take a short-term, short-sighted approach and mistake reactions for solutions, we will endanger our peaceful, democratic global coexistence.

Unfortunately, those who are actively working to destroy democratic structures and erode human rights are numerous, successful, and powerful. The 'strongmen' are the worst offenders. In his book *The Age of the Strongman*,[3] Gideon Rachman writes that Vladimir Putin is both the archetype and the model for the current generation of strongmen. He argues that the ubiquitous rise of these figures has fundamentally changed world politics and brought the most sustained global attack on liberal democratic values since the 1930s. Besides Putin, the strongmen identified by Rachman include Xi Jinping, Recep Tayyip Erdoğan, Viktor Orbán, Jair Bolsonaro, Donald Trump, Andrés Manuel López Obrador, Rodrigo Duterte, Narendra Modi – and I would now add Benjamin Netanyahu, Javier Milei,

J.D. Vance and Elon Musk. These populist and authoritarian figures, who scorn liberal and democratic values, currently play a defining role in world politics.

The authoritarian and in most cases far-right ideology behind many of these strongmen threatens people worldwide, particularly women and other political minorities. This is also true in Germany. While the danger emanating from the right and the far right seems to be increasingly well understood, much less attention is paid to the threat to women's rights. A survey by the market research institute Civey at the beginning of 2024 found that 48 per cent of the German population (more or less the same for both men and women) were *not* worried that the growing success of the AfD could reverse the progress already achieved in gender equality.[4]

Right-wing extremism and antifeminism are not isolated phenomena, but often go hand in hand. They share the notion of a supposedly 'natural' social order, in which traditional gender roles are firmly fixed and women play a subordinate role. And just as the family – according to the far-right narrative – needs a strong father, the country needs a strong political leader to guide and 'protect' the nation. Clearly, a large part of my resistance in the next few years will have to go into fighting (extreme) right-wing ideologies.

One of the basic principles of New Right and far-right politics is the rejection of feminism, of financial, social and physical freedom for women, and of diversity in women's lifestyles and family structures. These movements also deny the rights of the LGBTQI+ community and pour ridicule on gender studies (while fighting to suppress this discipline).

Ridicule and hostility towards feminists and gender mainstreaming do not appeal solely to extremists, nor do campaigns against sexual diversity and gender equality. They fall on fertile ground even in the mainstream, the centre: in Germany, one in three men and one in five women have a completely antifeminist worldview.[5]

Antifeminism is as old as the emancipatory movement of feminism itself. In the mid-nineteenth century, the fight for equal rights in the German empire met with fierce antifeminist reactions. Under the Nazis, women were reduced to their role as mothers and preservers of the 'national community' (*Volksgemeinschaft*). Homosexuality was branded as a danger for the population growth of the 'Aryan race'. In 1933 the Institute for Sexual Science, established by Magnus Hirschfeld (who was Jewish, gay and a socialist), was raided and shut down. These antifeminist policies and ideologies are still around today in various forms.

A deep-seated aversion towards (certain) women is the connective tissue between white supremacists, alt-right movements, right-wing extremists and their lesser-known subcultures such as the 'manosphere', which includes incels, men's rights activists and pickup artists. The building of hierarchies, in which women and 'femininity' rank below men and 'masculinity', is mixed with antisemitism and racism, especially in currently popular conspiracy ideologies. This mixture is a driving force for violence and terrorism.

The danger becomes especially obvious in the successful dissemination of a conspiracy narrative with far-right origins: that of the 'Great Replacement'. This is the fantasy that the government is deliberately replacing the white population with migrants. The tools for this replacement are, supposedly, falling birth rates among white women, rising birth rates in the migrant population, and liberal migration policy. The alleged culprits are feminism, which persuades women to have careers instead of children; access to safe abortions; and 'the Jews', who are accused of masterminding these developments. This narrative evokes a situation of legitimate self-defence, where the far right claim to be defending themselves (or the nation) against the 'weapon of migration' and those who deploy it, 'the Jews', but also against the 'agents' who help them. This draws attention to representatives of democratic civil society.

The extremely dangerous ideology of the 'Great Replacement' was found in the manifestos of the men who attacked a synagogue in Halle, Germany, and a mosque in Christchurch, New Zealand, both in 2019.[*]

When thinking about this subject, I can't help remembering the words of the great feminist writer Virginia Woolf: 'The history of men's opposition to women's emancipation is more interesting perhaps than the story of that emancipation itself.'[6] This form of opposition to the human rights and personal freedoms of a particular population group absolutely requires *our* resistance.

The world situation is more than critical. In March 2024 the German aid organization Brot für die Welt (Bread for the World) presented the latest figures from the *Atlas der Zivilgesellschaft* (Atlas of civil society). The figures showed that only 170 million people – around 2 per cent of the world's population – live in states where basic civil society freedoms, such as the freedom of opinion and freedom of assembly, are guaranteed. These are the thirty-seven countries that are classified as 'open' in the Civicus Monitor, on which the *Atlas* is based. In the 2024 *Atlas* Germany no longer falls into the 'open' category, but is classified as 'narrowed', particularly because of the way authorities and the justice system have dealt with climate activists. The UK's rating is even worse: it is classed as 'obstructed'. In 2023 the majority of the world's population lived in countries in which civil society was 'obstructed', 'repressed' or 'closed'. In these authoritarian states the governments restrict civil liberties and harass, arrest or persecute critics. This applies to 60 per cent of the world's countries.[7] For the first time in more than two decades, the world has

---

[*] My thoughts on the connection between antifeminism and far-right extremism were triggered by a talk I gave shortly before the European elections of 2024, at an event organized by CFFP. When working on my speech, I was supported by Judith Rahner, an expert on antifeminism and authoritarianism.

more closed autocracies than liberal democracies. There are 2.2 billion people living in closed autocracies, as opposed to around one billion in liberal democracies.[8] Faced with these global challenges, we must take political action for democracy, human rights, the preservation of our livelihoods, peace, and security for all. For this we need a clear and human-centred attitude: empathy. And we need to know when boundaries are being overstepped and when to say 'enough is enough'. This is resistance.

For both these things, this book seeks to give stimulation, conceptual clarity, and confidence.

And while the above-mentioned figures make me speechless for a moment, this doesn't last long. I take a breath, stand up straight and get to work.

This is what I want for all of us.

# Notes

## Chapter 1  How I found my compass

1 Maren Urner, *Radikal emotional: Wie Gefühle Politik machen* [Radically emotional: how feelings make politics], Munich: Droemer, 2024, p. 15.

2 Heidi Kastner, *Dummheit* [Stupidity], Vienna: Kremayr & Scheriau, 2021, p. 65.

3 See Kristina Lunz, 'Wie ich es als Arbeiterkind vom Dorf nach Oxford schaffte' [How I made it to Oxford as a working-class country girl], *ze.tt*, 4 November 2016.

4 Rebecca Traister, *Good and Mad: The Revolutionary Power of Women's Anger*, New York: Simon & Schuster, 2018, p. xxiii.

5 '"Bild" verabschiedet sich vom Oben-ohne-"Bild-Girl"' [*Bild* says goodbye to the topless *Bild* girl], *Süddeutsche Zeitung*, 12 March 2018.

6 Campaign website for #ausnahmslos, English version, https://ausnahmslos.org/english.

7 Kristina Lunz, 'Nein heißt nein!' [No means no!], *Zeit Online*, 8 March 2016.

8 Kim Stanley Robinson, *The Ministry for the Future*, London: Orbit Books, 2020, p. 35.

9 Bundesverband Frauenberatungsstellen und Frauennotrufe Frauen gegen Gewalt e. V. (ed.), 'Kampagne "Vergewaltigung Verurteilen"' [Campaign: rape convictions], https://www. frauen-gegen-gewalt.de/de/aktionen-themen/kampagnen/ver gewaltigung-verurteilen/zahlen-und-fakten-zum-plakat-ver gewaltigung-verurteilen.html.

10 Harvard Radcliffe Institute, 'Ruth Bader Ginsburg tells young women: "fight for the things you care about"', 6 February 2015, https://www.radcliffe.harvard.edu/news-and-ideas/ruth-bader -ginsburg-tells-young-women-fight-for-the-things-you-care -about.

11 V-Dem Institute, *Democracy Report 2024: Democracy Winning and Losing at the Ballot*, p. 6, https://www.v-dem.net/documents /43/v-dem_dr2024_lowres.pdf.

## Chapter 2 Empathy

1 Kastner, *Dummheit*, pp. 80ff.

2 Ibid., p. 86.

3 'Stephen Hawking calls aggression the human failing he'd most like to correct', *Huffington Post*, 19 February 2015.

4 Paul Bloom, *Against Empathy: The Case for Rational Compassion*, New York: Ecco, 2016.

5 Fritz Breithaupt, *Die dunklen Seiten der Empathie* [The dark sides of empathy], Frankfurt am Main: Suhrkamp, 2017, pp. 7, 11.

6 Ibid., p. 7.

7 Ibid., p. 109.

8 Ibid., p. 111.

9 The anecdote, widely shared on social media, is most often associated with the Christian pacifist A.J. Muste. No source can be found, but see, for example, https://www.spiritualityand practice.com/practices/naming-the-days/view/16580/a-j- muste-day.

10 Susan Neiman, *Left Is Not Woke*, Cambridge: Polity, 2023, pp. 11ff.

11  Ibid., pp. 26ff.

12  Michael Sfard, 'In Gaza, Israel is racing to the moral abyss', *Haaretz*, 23 October 2023.

13  Lisa Jaspers, Naomi Ryland and Silvie Horch (eds), *Unlearn Patriarchy*, Berlin: Ullstein, 2022.

14  Neiman, *Left Is Not Woke*, p. 143.

15  Kristina Lunz, Instagram post on 30 October 2023, https://www. instagram.com/p/CzCbDMoM0D5/.

16  Lena Gorelik, Miryam Schellbach and Mirjam Zadoff, 'Vorwort' [Preface], in Lena Gorelik, Miryam Schellbach and Mirjam Zadoff (eds), *Trotzdem sprechen* [Speaking nonetheless], Berlin: Ullstein, 2024, pp. 7–11, here pp. 7–8.

## Chapter 3  Resistance

1  Martin Luther King, Letter from Birmingham Jail, August 1963, https://www.csuchico.edu/iege/_assets/documents/susi-letter -from-birmingham-jail.pdf.

2  Antje Schrupp, Instagram post, 23 October 2023, https://www. instagram.com/p/CyvVi4Wob_Z/.

3  David P. Barash, *Out of Eden: The Surprising Consequences of Polygamy*, Oxford: Oxford University Press, 2016, p. 27.

4  Elizabeth Flock, *The Furies: Three Women and Their Violent Fight for Justice*, New York: Penguin, 2024, p. 3; Nimmi Gowrinathan, *Radicalizing Her: Why Women Choose Violence*, Boston: Beacon Press, 2021.

5  Centre for Feminist Foreign Policy, 'Über 100 namhafte Frauen aus Politik, Kultur und Wirtschaft fordern ihre Rechte ein: Dringender offener Brief an Justizminister Buschmann (FDP) und die Bundesregierung zu ihrer Blockade-Haltung zum EU-weiten Schutz von Millionen von Frauen vor Gewalt' [Over 100 well-known women from politics, culture and business demand their rights: urgent open letter to Justice Minister Buschmann (FDP) and the German federal government on their blockade of EU-wide protection aginst violence for millions of women], 29 January 2024, https://centreforfeministforeignpolicy

.org/2024/01/29/dringender-offener-brief-an-justizminister-buschmann/.

6   https://speakola.com/grad/ursula-le-guin-we-are-volcanoes-bryn-mawr-1986.

7   Andrea Kettenmann, *Frida Kahlo, 1907–1954: Pain and Passion*, Cologne: Taschen, 2003, p. 48.

8   Nir Eyal, 'Love is measured by the benefit of the doubt: the secret to true kindness', *Nir and Far*, https://www.nirandfar.com/secret-to-kindness/#:~:text=Everyone%20is%20just%20a%20grown,than%20attempts%20to%20hurt%20you.

9   Teaser from the publisher (KiWi) for Benjamin von Stuckrad-Barre's novel *Noch wach?* [Still awake?], https://www.kiwi-verlag.de/buch/benjamin-von-stuckrad-barre-noch-wach-97834623 11457.

10  Philipp Sterzer, *Die Illusion der Vernunft: Warum wir von unseren Überzeugungen nicht zu überzeugt sein sollten* [The illusion of reason: why we shouldn't be too convinced by our convictions], Berlin: Ullstein, 2022, pp. 250f.

11  Mirna Funk, *Von Juden lernen* [Learning from Jews], Berlin: dtv, 2024, pp. 122ff.

12  Ibid., p. 124.

13  Ibid., pp. 124ff.

14  Ibid., pp. 130f.

15  Ibid., p. 136.

16  Lyndsey Stonebridge, *We Are Free to Change the World: Hannah Arendt's Lessons in Love and Disobedience*, London: Jonathan Cape, 2024, p. 3.

17  Friedemann Karig, *Was ihr wollt: Wie Protest wirklich wirkt* [What you will: how protest really works], Berlin: Ullstein, 2024, p. 104.

18  Kristina Lunz, 'Neun Tipps für angehende Aktivist*innen' [Nine tips for budding activists], *ze.tt*, 8 March 2017.

## Chapter 4 The tools for empathy and resistance

1 Neiman, *Left Is Not Woke*, p. 92.
2 Rupi Kaur, 'Legacy', in *The Sun and Her Flowers*, Toronto: Simon & Schuster, 2017, p. 213.
3 *Disturbing the Peace: A Conversation with Karel Hvížďala*, New York: Vintage, 1990, trans. Paul Wilson, p. 181.
4 This paragraph is strongly inspired by Emilia Roig, *Why We Matter: Das Ende der Unterdrückung* [Why we matter: the end of oppression], Berlin: Aufbau Taschenbuch, 2021, pp. 108ff.
5 Nicole Seifert, *Frauen Literatur: Abgewertet, vergessen, wiederentdeckt* [Women's literature: denigrated, forgotten, rediscovered], Cologne: Kiepenheuer & Witsch, 2021.
6 Stonebridge, *We Are Free to Change the World* (including the quote from Arendt), pp. 228–9.

## Chapter 5 My compass in tempestuous times

1 Eva Menasse, *Alles und nichts sagen: Vom Zustand der Debatte in der Digitalmoderne* [Saying everything and nothing: on the state of debate in digital modernity], Cologne: Kiepenheuer & Witsch, 2023, p. 7.
2 Ibid., p. 15.
3 Heinz Bude, 'Das ganze Land muss den Schalter umlegen: Über die neue Wut in Deutschland' [The whole country has to flip the switch: on the new rage in Germany], *Das Polikteil* podcast, 12 January 2024.
4 Menasse, *Alles und nichts sagen*, p. 17.
5 Maryam Zaree, 'Träume' [Dreams], in Gorelik et al. (eds), *Trotzdem sprechen*, pp. 12–23, here p. 20.
6 Menasse, *Alles und nichts sagen*, p. 96.
7 Kristina Lunz, Instagram post from 8 October 2023, https://www.instagram.com/p/CyI_kFaMg7a/.
8 Breithaupt, *Die dunklen Seiten der Empathie*, p. 106.
9 Sven Becker et al., 'Der Chef der Münchner Sicherheitskonferenz und seine diskreten Geschäfte mit den Mächtigen' [The head of

the Munich Security Conference and his discreet deals with the powerful], *Der Spiegel*, 17 February 2022.

10 Heike Specht, *Die Ersten ihrer Art: Frauen verändern die Welt* [The first of their kind: women change the world], Munich: Piper, 2024, pp. 62ff.

11 Omri Boehm on 29 May 2024 at an event at Ullstein.

12 Asha Hedayati, 'Unlearn Recht' [Unlearn law], in Emilia Roig, Alexandra Zykunov and Silvie Horch (eds), *Unlearn Patriarchy 2*, Berlin: Ullstein, 2024, pp. 119–38, here pp. 119ff.

13 For example, 'Die Rammstein-Konzerte müssen abgesagt werden' [The Rammstein concerts must be cancelled], *Focus Online*, 9 June 2023.

14 Ibid.

15 'The 1% of the population accountable for 63% of all violent crime convictions', 31 October 2013, National Center for Biotechnology Information, https://www.ncbi.nlm.nih.gov/pmc/articles/PMC3969807/.

16 'Dunkelfeldstudie des Bundeskriminalamtes "Sicherheit und Kriminalität in Deutschland. SKiD 2020"' [Study on unreported crime by the German Federal Criminal Office, 'Security and Crime in Germany: SKiD 2020'], https://www.frauen-gegen-gewalt.de/de/infothek/gewalt-gegen-frauen/studienergebnisse/dunkelfeldstudie-skid-bka-2022.html.

17 Sebastian Kemnitzer and Lisabell Shewafera, 'Warum werden so wenige Täter verurteilt?' [Why are so few offenders convicted?], *tagesschau.de*, 1 November 2019.

18 Julian Dörr, 'Der Mythos der falschen Beschuldigung' [The myth of the false accusation], *Süddeutsche Zeitung*, 12 October 2018.

19 See also the subchapter on 'feminist international law' in my book *The Future of Foreign Policy is Feminist*, pp. 104–11.

20 Brené Brown, *Dare to Lead: Brave Work. Tough Conversations. Whole Hearts*, London: Random House, 2018, p. 20.

## Chapter 6  Women of empathy and resistance

1 Kristina Lunz, 'Abtreibungsreferendum: Warum britische Universitäten irischen Studierenden Geld für die Heimreise zahlen' [Abortion referendum: why British universities are paying Irish students money to travel home], *ze.tt*, 25 May 2018.

2 Guen Murroni, 'Under Irish law, a woman who seeks an abortion after rape can face a longer prison sentence than her rapist – but this could be about to change', *The Independent Online*, 14 December 2017.

3 Nadja Al-Khalaf, '5 Dinge, die ihr über Schwangerschaftsabbrüche in Irland wissen solltet' [Five things you should know about abortion in Ireland], *ze.tt*, 7 May 2018.

4 HÁWAR.help (ed.), '9. Jahrestag Genozid an den Jesiden. Unsere Forderungen' [9th anniversary of the genocide of the Yazidis: our demands], 28 July 2023, https://www.hawar.help/de/neunter-jahrestag-forderungen/.

5 Johanna Adorján in an interview with Düzen Tekkal, 'Ich lasse mich nicht einschüchtern' [I won't be intimidated], *Süddeutsche Zeitung*, 4 January 2024.

6 *Live to Lead: Gloria Steinem*, dir. Geoff Blackwell, Netflix, 2022. https://www.netflix.com/gb/title/81406763.

7 Ibid.

8 Gloria Steinem, *My Life on the Road*, New York: Random House, 2015, p. xix.

9 Ibid., p. xxiii.

10 Ibid., p. 37.

11 Geoff Blackwell (ed.), *Gloria Steinem: I Know This to Be True: On Integrity, Empathy and Authenticity*, San Francisco: Chronicle Books, 2020, p. 19.

12 Steinem, *My Life on the Road*, p. 23.

13 Ibid., p. 28.

14 Written interview via email, 19 February 2025.

## Chapter 7 Why empathy and resistance are so important now

1 Sarfraz Manzoor, 'She's Israeli, he's an Arab. War has made them like mother and son', *The Guardian*, 10 May 2009.

2 Brené Brown, 'Ali Abu Awwad and Robi Damelin on nonviolence as the path to freedom for Palestinians and Israelis', *Unlocking Us* podcast, 28 February 2024.

3 Gideon Rachman, *The Age of the Strongman: How the Cult of the Leader Threatens Democracy Around the World*, New York: Bodley Head, 2022.

4 https://app.civey.com/dashboards/frauen100-17612.

5 Oliver Decker, Johannes Kiess, Ayline Heller and Elmar Brähler (eds), *Autoritäre Dynamiken in unsicheren Zeiten: Neue Herausforderungen – alte Reaktionen? (Leipziger Autoritarismus-Studie 2022)* [Authoritarian dynamics in uncertain times: New challenges – old reactions? (Leipzig study on authoritarianism 2022)], https://www.theol.uni-leipzig.de/fileadmin/ul/Doku mente/221109_Leipziger-Autoritarismus-Studie.pdf.

6 Virginia Woolf, *A Room of One's Own*, London: Vintage, 2018 [1929], p. 74.

7 'CIVICUS-Monitor: Atlas der Zivilgesellschaft 2024' [CIVICUS monitor: atlas of civil society 2024], https://www.brot-fuer-die -welt.de/themen/atlas-der-zivilgesellschaft/. See also https:// monitor.civicus.org/globalfindings_2024/.

8 V-Dem Institute, *Democracy Report 2023*, https://www.v-dem .net/documents/29/V-dem_democracyreport2023_lowres.pdf.